VOLUME #7

BY

MINE YOSHIZAKI

HAMBURG // LONDON // LOS ANGELES // TOKYO

SGT. Frog Vol. 7

Created by Mine Yoshizaki

Translation - Yuko Fukami
English Adaptation - Carol Fox
Associate Editor - Aaron Sparrow
Retouch and Lettering - Jeannie Lee
Production Artist - James Dashiell and Jose Macasocol, Jr.
Cover Design - Raymond Makowski

Editor - Paul Morrissey
Digital Imaging Manager - Chris Buford
Pre-Press Manager - Antonio DePietro
Production Managers - Jennifer Miller and Mutsumi Miyazaki
Art Director - Matt Alford
Managing Editor - Jill Freshney
VP of Production - Ron Klamert
Editor-in-Chief - Mike Kiley
President and C.O.O. - John Parker
Publisher and C.E.O. - Stuart Levy

TOKYOPOP Inc.
5900 Wilshire Blvd. Suite 2000
Los Angeles, CA 90036

E-mail: info@TOKYOPOP.com
Come visit us online at www.TOKYOPOP.com

ISBN: 1-59532-448-8

First TOKYOPOP printing: March 2005

10 9 8 7 6 5 4 3 2

Printed in the USA

RELATIONSHIP BETWEEN THE CHARACTERS AND SUMMARY OF THE STORY

(RESEARCHED BY MAGAZINE SHONEN ACE)

AKI HINATA

FUYUKI HINATA

THE FIFTH ONE

+

?

MOMOKA NISHIZAWA

NATSUMI HINATA

DARK MOMOKA

SERGEANT KERORO

PRIVATE TAMAMA

CORPORAL GIRORO

KOGORO 556

RABBIE

ANGOL MOA

FIRST SERGEANT KULULU

MUTSUMI

ABSOLUTE SUBMISSION

ABSOLUTE SUBMISSION

RECREATIONAL [HEALING] PET

ABSOLUTE SUBMISSION

NERVOUS, UNREQUITED LOVE

(ONE-SIDED)

A RELATIONSHIP BASED ON... TRUST?

?

NO INTEREST WHATSOEVER

ABSOLUTE SUBMISSION

METAMORPHOSIS

MULTIPLE PERSONALITY BUDDIES

HARD-BOILED LOVE

A MAIDEN...

AN UNEXPECTED KINSHIP

REVERENCE

CHILDHOOD FRIENDS

SUGAR DADDY

DANGEROUS FRIENDS

CAT AND DOG

RIVALRY FOR THE SERGEANT'S LOVE

RIVALS IN LOVE

SIBLING LOVE

WAVE BUDDIES

BEAUTY AND THE BEAST

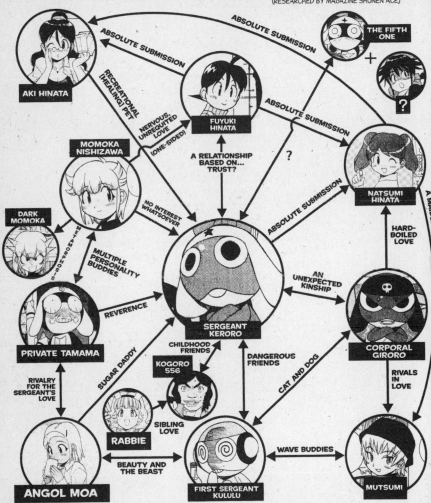

AS CAPTAIN OF THE SPACE INVASION FORCE'S SPECIAL ADVANCE TEAM OF THE 58TH PLANET OF THE GAMMA STORM CLOUD SYSTE SGT. KERORO ENTERED THE HINATA FAMILY WHEN HIS PRE-ATTACK PREPARATION FOR THE INVASION OF EARTH RAN AFOUL VIA HIS EASY CAPTURE BY THE HINATA CHILDREN, FUYUKI AND NATSUMI. THANKS TO FUYUKI'S KINDNESS, OR AT LEAST HIS CURIOSITY, SGT. KERORO QUICKLY BECAME A BONA FIDE MEMBER OF THE HINATA FAMILY...IN OTHER WORDS, A TOTAL FREELOADER. THE SERGEANT'S SUBORDINATES--"DUAL PERSONALITY" PRIVATE TAMAMA; "BLAZING MILITARY MAN" CORPORATE GIRORO; THE "WAVISH" FIRST SERGEAN KULULU; AND THE MUCH-HERALDED "LORD OF TERROR," ANGOL MOA--SOON JOINED HIM TO REFORM THE KERORO PLATOON, WHICH DOE AS IT PLEASES IN A TOP-SECRET BASE BENEATH THE HINATA HOME. THUS HAVE THEIR OBNOXIOUS DAYS CONTINUED...

AND AT LAST--THE LONG-AWAITED FIFTH ONE APPEARS! WILL THE INVASION OF EARTH FINALLY GO FORWARD?!

A week has passed...

...but I'm spending the days as usual.

...and maybe I haven't gotten used to it...

FUYUKI!! DO YOUR WORK. NO SLACKING OFF!!

OKAY.

HYAAA! IT'S COLD!!

IT'S ALMOST WINTER...

ENCOUNTER LIV
THE WORLD'S SMALLEST INVASION: CONTINUED

WHAT ARE YOU DOING HERE?
mew?

meow
meow

meow meow

THERE'S NOTHING TO DIG FOR THERE.
SILLY CAT.
JUST DON'T EVER COME HERE WHEN MOM IS HOME!
SHE REALLY HATES ANIMALS ...

C'MON-- SCOOT ALREADY!
meowww

THAT'S WHY WE'VE NEVER HAD...
...ANY PETS... I GUESS.

WHAT I WOULDN'T GIVE FOR A NICE, GOLDEN, COOKED TO A "T"...
OH, NO. I'M THINKING ABOUT ROASTED SWEET POTATOES AGAIN.
BUT...
...IS IT REALLY JUST POTATOES...?
IS IT GONE?
IT'S GONE.
COM-PLETELY?
YES... WITHOUT A TRACE.
OH, BOY... AM I EVER IN A BIND.

I'M REALLY UP SHIT CREEK NOW!

DIDN'T EXPECT HEAD-QUARTERS TO CALL US BACK SO SUDDENLY.

BUT... AT LEAST WE'RE BACK SAFELY!!

Gero Gero Gero Gero Gero Gero Gero Gero

WHAT DO YOU MEAN, SAFELY? DO YOU REALIZE HOW MUCH PLEADING AND CONNING I HAD TO DO?

THIS IS ALL BECAUSE OF YOUR SPINELESS-NESS...

MILITARY LAW NUMBER 4: "UPON LEAVING A PLANET, ALL MEMORIES OF ALIEN CONTACT MUST BE RETURNED TO THEIR INITIAL CONDITION."

IT SEEMS TO HAVE WORKED PERFECTLY... KU, KU, KU, KU...

HEY! DOES THAT MEAN MOMOTCHI HAS FORGOTTEN ABOUT ME, TOO?

AWW... I NEED SOME POKOPENIAN CANDY, QUICK!

I SEE...SO THE HINATA FAMILY HAS NO MEMORY OF OUR EXISTENCE AT ALL...
THAT MEANS NATSUMI'S FORGOTTEN ABOUT ME, AS WELL.
WE'RE NO LONGER THEIR HOSTAGES ...
ISN'T IT BETTER THIS WAY? KU, KU, KU, KU...
NATSUMI'S FORGOTTEN ME... NATSUMI'S FORGOTTEN ME... NATSUMI'S FORGOTTEN ME... NATSUMI'S FORGOTTEN ME...

WE'LL FINALLY BE ABLE TO CONCENTRATE ON INVADING POKEPEN, OLD MAN!!
KU, KU, KU, KU, KU, KU!
KU, KU, KU, KU, KU, KU!

DOES THAT MEAN WE'RE STARTING FROM ZERO?

......

MASTER FUYUKI...

I WONDER IF I'LL HAVE TO RE-COLLECT ALL MY *GUNDAM* MODELS... Sigh...

?

THIS IS ALL YOUR FAULT!!!

AIEEEEE?!

OH... UH...
Awkward!♥
HELLO. I'M AN ALIEN.
S...

SERGEANT!!
A WHOLE WEEK... I MISSED YOU!!
WHERE HAVE YOU BEEN?!
Gero?
I-I'M SORRY?!
WHAT'S HAPPEN-ING?!
THEIR MEMORIES-- IT MUST BE--?!

KU, KU, KU KU...
PUSH
IT'S FOR TIMES LIKE THESE THAT ONE...
...HAS BACKUPS.

YOU!
Sigh...
THAT'S WORTH A COURT-MARTIAL.

I'M HOOOME!! ♪

MOM!! AND...
...NISHI-ZAWA-SAN!
WE RAN INTO EACH OTHER. ♡
I THOUGHT MAYBE TAMA-CHAN WAS HERE...
THAT'S IT! GOOD OPENING LINE!!

YAY! IT'S MOMOTCHI!
TAMA-CHAN!
IDIOT! I WANTED TO TALK TO FUYUKI!!
BUT, MOM-- WHAT ABOUT WORK?
I GOT OFF AT LUNCH TODAY!
ONE OF THE PERKS OF BEING HALF-FREELANCE. ♡

TONIGHT I'M GONNA MAKE MOM'S SPECIAL DINNER!!
REALLY?!
YAHOO!! EXCELLENT TIMING, I SAY!!
OH, STUPID FROOOG!

I'LL TEACH YOU TO SKIP OUT ON YOUR DUTIES FOR A WHOLE WEEK...
AND LET'S SEE... I'M GONNA NEED THE RED ONE!!
Meow!
THE YELLOW ONE!!
KU, KU...
AND THE BLACK ONE, TOO!!
I'M GONNA WORK ALL OF YOU 'TIL YOU DROP!!
KyAAAAAH!

AND SO, AT EARTH TIME 1:12 P.M., ON THE FOURTH SUNDAY OF NOVEMBER...

...THE KERON FORCE'S "OPERATION: POKOPEN INVASION" RESUMED!

AND THE EARTH ITSELF...
...LOOKED A LITTLE BIT ANNOYED!
THIS AIN'T OVER...
MUST BIDE OUT TIME JUST A BIT LONGER... KU, KU, KU, KU...
TO BE CONTINUED

ENCOUNTER LV
ENTER THE DRAGONLIKE TRANSFER STUDENT!

ENCOUNTER LV ENTER THE DRAGONLIKE TRANSFER STUDENT!

ALL RIGHT. NEXT!
AND-- NEXT!
YOU'RE TOO STIFF!
OOF!
OKAY, NEXT!
DO YOU LIKE P.E., KOYUKI-CHAN?
P.E.?
OH! YOU MEAN THE PHYSICAL ARTS? YES...VERY MUCH!
AH HA HA! I GUESS YOU COULD CALL IT THAT, IF YOU WANNA BE OLD-FASHIONED!
YOU'RE UP, HINATA-SAN.
OKAY!

FROM A ROUND-OFF...

...A BACK-TURN TWIST!!!

WOW, NATSUMI! YOU'RE AMAZING! ♡
SHE COULD MAKE IT TO THE NATIONAL ATHLETIC MEET!
WOWWW...

AM I SUPPOSED TO DO THAT?
NO, NO. THAT WAS NATSUMI'S SPECIALTY.
JUST DO A FORWARD TURN. DON'T PUSH YOUR-SELF TOO HARD.

CITY KIDS ARE PRETTY GOOD...
...BUT I CAN'T LET THEM WIN!
SMILE
NEXT UP-- AMAZUYA-SAN!
HERE!
GO, KOYUKI-CHAN!
UMM...
VERTICAL THREE-TURN TWIST...
TAP
!!!

silence

IN...
Eh heh...
W-WAS IT THAT BAD?

HUH...?

...INCREDIBLE, KOYUKI-CHAN!!!
SERIOUSLY-- WHAT WAS THAT?! IT WAS LIKE THE OLYMPICS!!
HEY-- A RIVAL FOR NATSUMI?!
NO WAY... I COULDN'T POSSIBLY DO ANYTHING LIKE THAT!!

THAT TRANSFER STUDENT WAS PRETTY AMAZING!
REALLY?

YEAH--I THINK THIS IS THE FIRST TIME IN A WHILE I'VE ACTUALLY BEEN SURPRISED BY A HUMAN BEING!
THAT'S TRUE-- WE'RE ALWAYS BEING SURPRISED BY ALIENS.
THOUGH NOT IN THE SAME WAY, I GUESS...

TAP

NATSUMI HINATA-CHAN...
...AND HER DARLING LITTLE BROTHER.
OH, YES, I CAN SMELL IT!
I KNOW THAT SMELL...
すんっ
すんっ
FOUND YA!
HEY THERE, CUTIE PIE!
WHAT'S A LI'L THING LIKE YOU DOING IN A DUMP LIKE THIS?
WHA ...?!
HI. I'M 623.♪
......?

shield
623
WHOA! THAT WAS UN-EXPECTED!!
WHAT HAPPENED?!
AND... WHAT'S THIS?
HMM...
...I GUESS THERE STILL ARE A LOT OF INTERESTING FOLKS LEFT IN THIS WORLD.

WELL, WELL, WELL, WELL.

THIS IS REALLY A TERRIBLE PROBLEM!!!

I AM IN A PRIME POSITION TO CREATE AN INVASION PLAN. HOWEVER...
...AS OF LATE, MY NUMBER OF UNASSEMBLED PLASTIC MODELS HAS INCREASED!
IF ACTION IS NOT TAKEN, I WILL DEVELOP A REPUTATION AS A "PACK FROG." THIS IS NOT GOOD! NOPE!! NOT GOOD AT ALL!

GLANCE

SO...WHAT TO DO FIRST? URRGHH... WELL... IF I MUST...

PLAST-- NO--POKOPEN... HMMMM...

NO! THEY'RE BOTH TOO IMPORTANT!! I CAN'T POSSIBLY CHOOSE!!

I KNOW! I SHALL LET THE DICE CHOOSE! YES--OUR FATE WILL DEPEND ON WHICH NUMBER IS ROLLED!!

IF IT'S ⚀ ⚁ OR ⚂ POKOPEN INVASION! IF IT'S ⚃ ⚄ OR ⚅ PLASTIC MODELS!!

WHOA!! NOW THAT'S WHAT I CALL A FAIR SYSTEM!!

OF COURSE... NATURALLY I WILL WANT TO ROLL A ⚀ ⚁ OR ⚂ SINCE WORK IS SO IMPORTANT!

Come onnnn... Come onnnn...

(WITHOUT PASSION!)

Whoa!

OH HO HO! A PAIR OF 4-5-6 DICE. PRETTY DECENTLY MADE, TOO.

456 DICE!!

表 FRONT

裏 BACK

WITH THESE, NO MATTER HOW MANY THOUSANDS OF TIMES YOU ROLL, YOU'LL NEVER ROLL A ⚀ ⚁ OR ⚂ ...

Uh... Ah... Um... Eep...

F-FUNNY. I HAD NO IDEA...
Doesn't count! Doesn't count!
I WONDER HOW THOSE GOT THERE? NO--THEY MUST HAVE WANDERED IN! THAT'S IT!
KERORO ...
CRUNCH
HAVEN'T YOU FORGOTTEN SOMETHING IMPORTANT?
GERO?
サララ...

SOMEONE IMPORTANT?!
しーーん。。
HUH...?

SILENCE

HOW AWKWARD. NO...NOT NOW...
IT'LL JUST CREATE AN AWKWARD SCENE. HE SHOULD JUST PRETEND TO HAVE FORGOTTEN.
Reading the same panel over and over.

YOU CAN'T READ THE AIR, CAN YOU, OLD MAN...?
KU, KU, KU, KU, KU...

WELL... THAT IS... UMMM...
THAT'S RIGHT.

ACK!
ALL THE OTHER SPECIES THAT ARE PLANNING TO INVADE POKOPEN!!!
HUH?
I NEED HARDLY STRESS THAT THOUSANDS...
...OF OTHER SPECIES HAVE POKOPEN IN THEIR SIGHTS!!

I COULDN'T STAND IT IF WE WERE BEATEN TO IT!!
UH... UMM...
WHAT ?!

SO... THIS FOR-GOTTEN THING...
...WAS THAT IT?
WHAT? WHAT ELSE IS THERE?!

OH, WELL...
LOOKS LIKE THE RED DHARMA HAS FOR-GOTTEN, TOO.

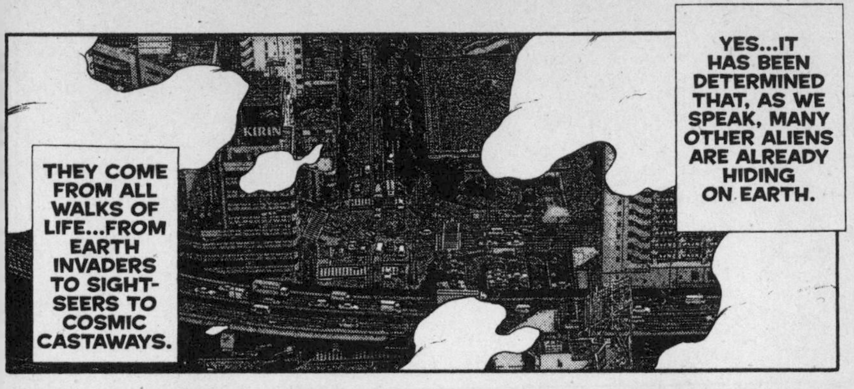

YES...IT HAS BEEN DETERMINED THAT, AS WE SPEAK, MANY OTHER ALIENS ARE ALREADY HIDING ON EARTH.
KIRIN
THEY COME FROM ALL WALKS OF LIFE...FROM EARTH INVADERS TO SIGHT-SEERS TO COSMIC CASTAWAYS.

CATTLE MUTI-LATORS... ABDUC-TORS... CROP CIRCLERS.

WE HAVE INTRO-DUCED SEVERAL CASES IN THIS BOOK ALONE.

Cosmic Criminal

POYO!

Cosmic X Soldier

Cosmic Policewoman Poyon

RICE...

Cosmic Cavity Bacteria Super Dali

IT TASTES GOOD, KOGORO!

HA HA HA HA HA HA!

Cosmic Detectives 556 & Rabbie

EVERY DAY, THEY ACTIVELY ENGAGE IN VARIOUS NEFARIOUS SCHEMES ON EARTH.

EVEN NOW... UN-DETECTED BY US...
LOOK! THERE!!
HEY! THERE HE IS!
HE'S SO CUTE!!

LOOK AT THIS CROWD!!

THEY'RE ALL HERE TO SEE JAPAN'S NEWEST IDOL...

THERE HE IS-- GESU-CHAN!!*

AWW... HOW CUUUUTE!!!

* Gesu means "vulgar" in Japanese.

* Gesui means "sewer" in Japanese.

BOW DOWN BEFORE MY IRRESISTIBLE CHARM!! WAH HA HA HA HA!!
YES! SHOWER ME WITH PRAISE!! GO CRAZY WITH LOVE!! COLLECT ALL MY LICENSED GOODS!!
SISEALIAN
SEAL-SHAPED ALIEN
GESU, GESU, GESU ...
FOOLISH POKO-PENIANS.
Ah ha!
Ah ha ha!
SPROING
KYAAAA!!
!!
GAKKKKK!
?

WHAT THE HELL IS THAT THING?!
IT'S SO VULGAR!
Waaah!!
NO! DON'T LOOK!
DAMMIT-- WHO'S RESPONSIBLE FOR THIS?!
!!
YOU ARE...?!
AN INCREDIBLE THING HAS HAPPENED!!
GESU-CHAN WAS REALLY A **PERVERT**!!
POOF

* Jama in Japanese means "nuisance."

!?

KASHAAAAH!
UH-OH.
WAAAAH!
STUDIO IN COMMOTION!!!

EEK!
WHAT THE HELL KIND OF PC IS THIS?!
SHOOM
OUR PHONES ARE RINGING OFF THE HOOK WITH COMPLAINTS!

TEE-HEE!

ELSE-WHERE IN TOKYO ...
...IN THE BATHROOM OF A VERY SEXY WOMAN ...
SHO WER...
SHOWER
Oh Yeah!
BOUNCY BOOB! FANTASTIC! ♪
SHOWER
Dear me!
TOTALLY NUDE-- MARVELOUS! ♪
....
TURN...
OH, GAWD...
WHENEVER I SHAMPOO, I ALWAYS FEEL LIKE THERE'S SOMEONE BEHIND ME. ♪
HMM... ♪
HMM... ♪

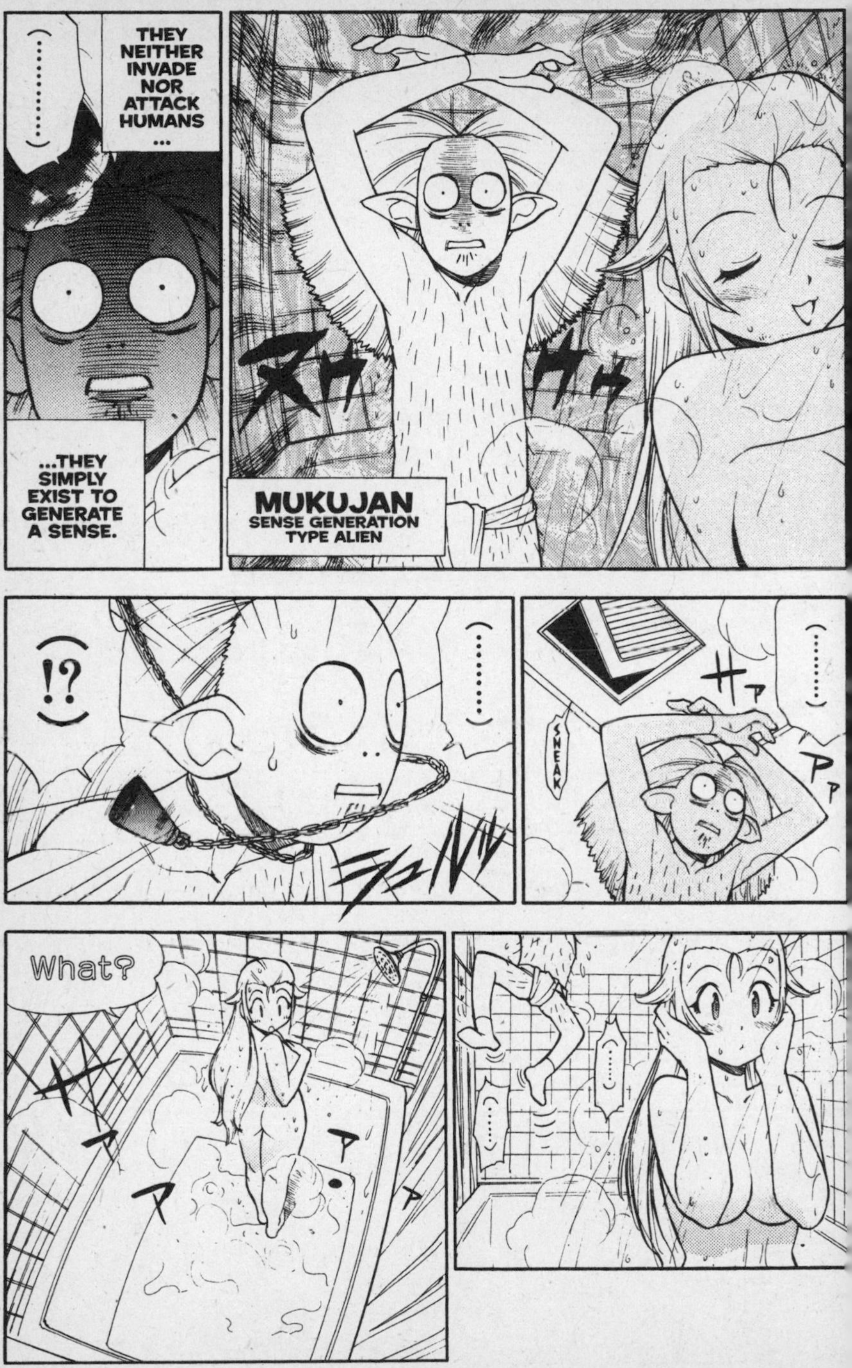

(.........)

THEY NEITHER INVADE NOR ATTACK HUMANS ...

...THEY SIMPLY EXIST TO GENERATE A SENSE.

MUKUJAN
SENSE GENERATION TYPE ALIEN

!?

(.........)

SNEAK

(.........)

What?

(.....)

(.....)

THE NEXT DAY...
DING DONG
COMING!
WHO IS IT?

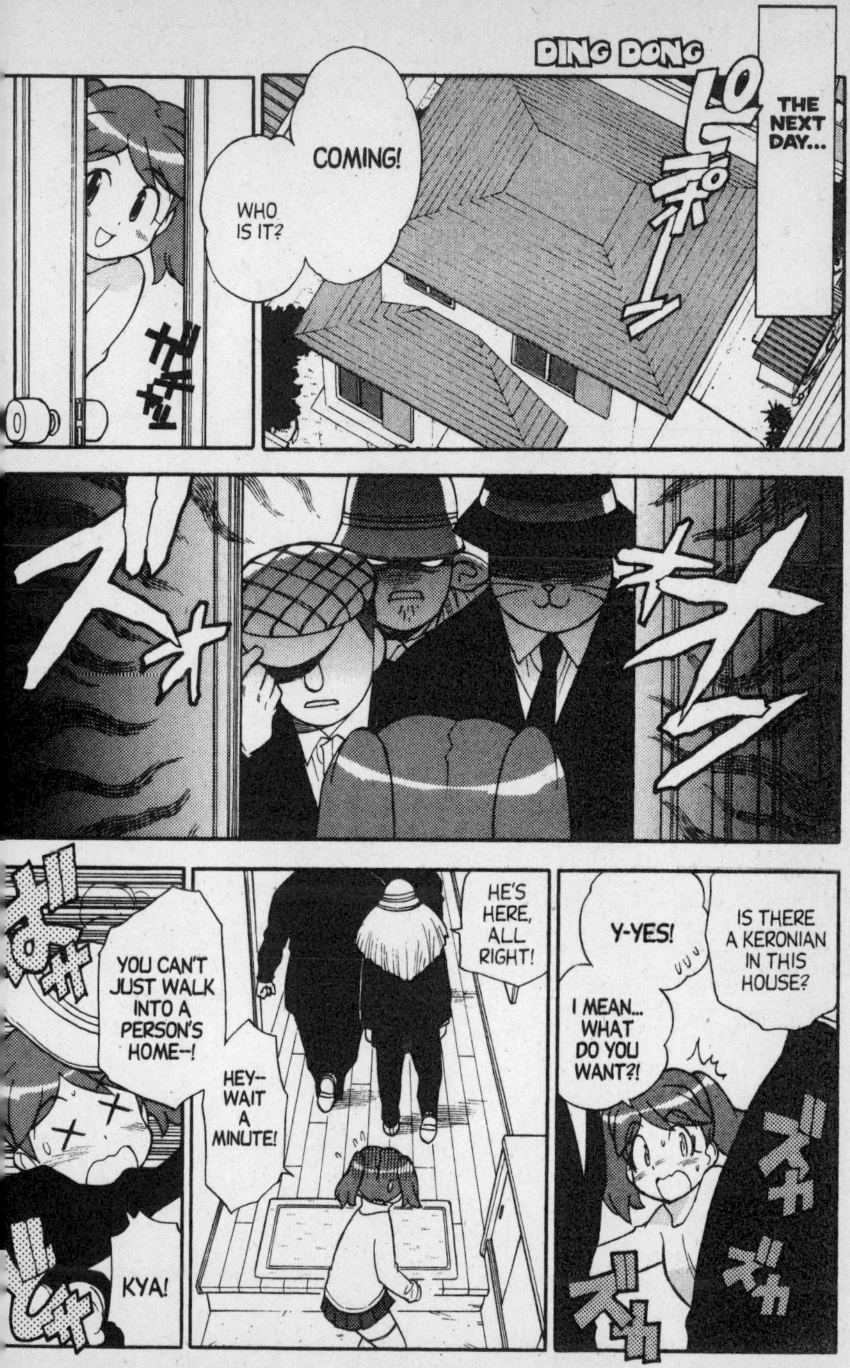

IS THERE A KERONIAN IN THIS HOUSE?

Y-YES!

I MEAN... WHAT DO YOU WANT?!

HE'S HERE, ALL RIGHT!

HEY-- WAIT A MINUTE!

YOU CAN'T JUST WALK INTO A PERSON'S HOME--!

KYA!

NOOOOOO!!!
ずん!

WE EMPHATICALLY PROTEST!!!

WE'RE NOT SUPPOSED TO HAVE ENEMY RELATIONS!!
INTERFERENCE WITH ANOTHER SPECIES' ACTIVITIES IS PROHIBITED BY COSMIC UNIVERSAL REGULATIONS!!

HOW DARE YOU STAND IN THE WAY OF MY SELLING SUPERIOR PRODUCTS AT A COMPETITIVE PRICE?!
MY FIRST CHANCE... TO BECOME... A POPULAR IDOL!!
(Generat-ing a sense of anger.)

W-WAIT A MINUTE! PLEASE... CALM DOWN!
WHAT IS THIS ALL ABOUT?!
WHAT ?!

YOU DENY EVERYTHING, THEN?

WELL, THAT JUST AIN'T GONNA FLY!

Gross...

GET A LOAD OF-- THESE!!

NO MATTER HOW YOU LOOK AT IT-- IT'S GOTTA BE ONE OF YOU KERONIANS!!

......

OH--THAT WAS DONE ON ONE OF OUR PRINTERS. ISN'T THE OUTPUT BEAUTIFUL?!

THE FIFTH MEMBER...?

SEE? YOU'RE DEAD MEAT!!

AT LEAST, YOU MUST CONFESS-- TO THAT HIGH QUALITY PRINT!!

NOW... WE'LL MAKE YOU ANSWER FOR WHAT YOU'VE DONE...

SPLAT

!!?

!!

IT HAS BEEN A WHILE...

I FEEL... ALMOST... NOSTALGIC.

CHINK

CAPTAIN, SIR!

ZE--

CORPORAL ZERORO!!!

WH-WHERE HAVE YOU BEEN?! I WAS SO WORRIED--REALLY!
YES!
YEAH, YEAH-- OH BOY-- I'LL SAY!!
WITH A LIGHT COMIC TOUCH, WE'LL DANCE AROUND THE AWKWARD-NESS!!
NOW THAT ALL FIVE OF US ARE HERE-- LET'S ALL RESONATE!!
WITH REGRET... I MUST DECLINE.
HUH?
Gero ... IS... IS HE MAD...
...AFTER ALL...?
WHY IS HE HERE NOW?!
I MEAN, WE'RE ALREADY ON THE SEVENTH VOLUME!
I MUST MAKE TWO CORREC-TIONS, CAPTAIN, SIR.
Y-YES? WHAT MIGHT THOSE BE?!
FIRSTLY, MY NAME.
I HAVE RID MYSELF OF THAT DETEST-ABLE MONIKER.
I AM NO LONGER ZERORO-- BUT DORORO!
AND SECONDLY ...
...GOOD-BYE, EX-CAPTAIN, SIR!!!
OHWAAAAH?!!

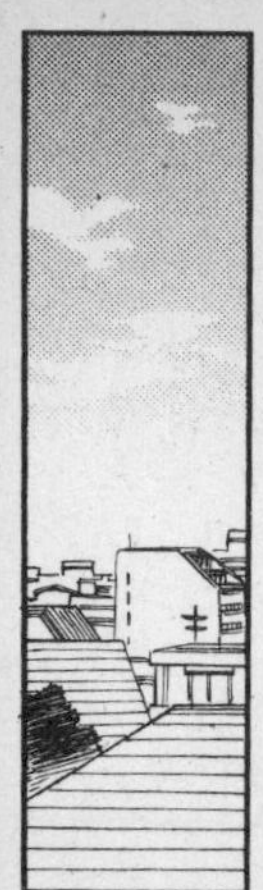

SO... HOW WERE YOUR OLD FRIENDS?

YOU HAVE ME TO THANK FOR FINDING THEM.

TAP

I AM GRACIOUS.

SMILE

AWAY WE GO, MASTER KOYUKI!

OFF TO PROTECT THIS BEAUTIFUL PLANET--EARTH!

AT LAST--THE FIFTH TROOPER, CORPORAL DORORO, HAS APPEARED!! BUT WHAT IS THE TRUTH BEHIND THIS MYSTERIOUS KERONIAN?!

TO BE CONTINUED

ENCOUNTER LVI
THE FIFTH ONE APPEARS! THE LEGEND OF DORORO

WHAT?! THE FIFTH MEMBER?! HE'S HERE?!

REALLY?! REALLY?!

VERY INTERESTED!

NOT "HE"--IT!
SO YOUR TROOPS ARE ALL FINALLY HERE?!
OH-- COULD YOU PLEASE-- MAYBE-- INTRODUCE ME?!

WELL, UH...
ちらっ
UMM...

HE ALREADY LEFT... PIPING MAD.
UH... YES.

WELL, HOW CAN YOU BLAME HIM? YOU NEGLECTED HIM FOR SO LONG...
AH-YAA. SUCH A FRANK OPINION FROM THE POKOPENIAN!!
THE THIRD PARTY HAS NO PROBLEM BEING STRAIGHT-FORWARD!

HMPH! NO LESS THAN YOU DESERVE!
I GET THE CREEPS EVERY TIME ONE OF YOU GUYS POPS UP, ANYWAY!
SO...WHAT DOES THE FIFTH ONE LOOK LIKE?
She is curious!
HUH?
WELL, UM...
TAMAMA DOESN'T KNOW VERY MUCH ABOUT HIM.
YOU SEE, TAMAMA AND KULULU JOINED US AFTER THE UNIT WAS ORIGINALLY FORMED.
ONLY GIRORO AND I KNEW ZERORO BEFORE THAT.
WE WERE CLASSMATES SINCE ELEMENTARY TRAINING SCHOOL*.
AND SO THE SER-GEANT ...
...WITH MISTY EYES...
...BEGAN TO SPEAK OF THE DAYS "BACK THEN."

* The Earth equivalent of Elementary School.

PLANET KERON!
BACK THEN!
Aaah!
Gyaaa! Gyaaa!
SPEED! SPEED! SPEED! SPEED! SPEED! SPEED!
SO MUCH SPEED! I AM SPEED!
KERORO (AND GIRORO): THE EARLY YEARS
WAIT FOR ME, KERORO-KUN!
TOO SLOW, ZERORO!!
pant
gasp
gag
ZERORO: THE EARLY YEARS
Zeroro was frail... always behind the rest of the class.
And he was shy too, so he didn't have many friends.
But for some reason, he always ended up playing with us ...
ZERORO-KUN!
LET'S PLAY!

WELCOME, KERORO. PLEASE-- COME IN.

WHOOAAA...

ZERORO-KUN, YOU'RE RICH!!

OH, NOT REALLY. WE'RE JUST REGULAR FOLKS.

ZERORO, DEAR...ARE THESE YOUR FRIENDS?

WELCOME, WELCOME!

OH-- HELLO!

THANK YOU SO MUCH FOR BEING ZERORO'S FRIENDS. THANK YOU... THANK YOU.
ST-STOP IT, MOTHER-- STOP!

LET'S GO UP TO MY ROOM.
WOWWWW !!!

WOW! ORIGINAL NINTENDO "GAME & WATCH" HANDHELDS FROM POKOPEN! LOOKIT ALL THIS STUFF!!
I BELIEVE I HAVE THEM ALL.
SO... MANY... TOYS...

....
PLAY AS MUCH AS YOU PLEASE.

AFTER ALL... WE'RE FRIENDS!
YES... FRIENDS...
BEST FRIENDS... RIGHT?
WOOOOO!
WHAT A THRILLING DOWNHILL RIDE!!
AWRIGHT-- NO MORE BRAKES FROM HERE ON!
WHAT?!
BUT-- BUT I'M SCARED, KERORO-KUN!!
IF YOU BREAK THE RULE, WE'RE NO LONGER FRIENDS!! THAT'S IT!!
SCARED...I'M SCARED...BUT SINCE WE'RE FRIENDS...
...SINCE WE'RE FRIENDS...
ACK!
I LIED!!!
BRAKES ARE OKAY! A-OKAY!!!

ZE-ZERO-RO ...?
HEEEE!
Due to these, er, circumstances ...

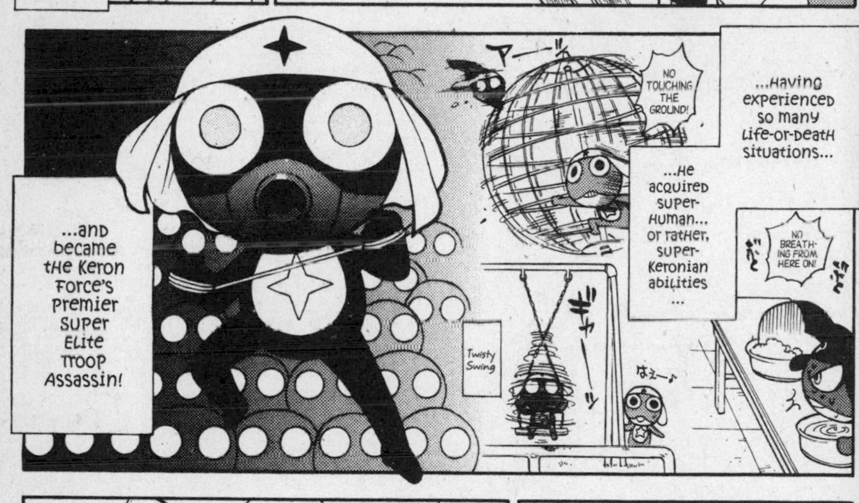
...Having experienced so many Life-or-Death situations...
NO TOUCHING THE GROUND!
...He acquired super-Human... or rather, super-Keronian abilities ...
NO BREATHING FROM HERE ON!
ギャーーッ
Twisty Swing
...and became the Keron Force's Premier Super Elite Troop Assassin!

しんみり
......
......

CAN YOU REALLY CALL THAT "BEING FRIENDS"?
I DON'T THINK SO.
B-BUT... WHAT ARE YOU SAYING? NO...THAT CAN'T BE RIGHT...

WELL, ZERORO...

I MEAN, DORORO...

...MAY HAVE BROKEN AWAY. BUT...

...TO BE QUITE HONEST, HIS SOLO FIGHTING ABILITY **FAR EXCEEDS MINE.**

WE'LL JUST HAVE TO **PRAY** HE DOESN'T TURN AGAINST US.

UNBEARABLE SILENCE...

耐え難き沈黙…。

SOUNDS LIKE THINGS ARE PRETTY MESSED UP.

WELL, TAKE CARE OF YOUR **OWN MESS YOURSELVES,** OKAY?!

BUT YOU BETTER GET THIS MATTER RESOLVED BEFORE IT AFFECTS **MY** LIFE!

SLAM

WOW. LOOKS LIKE THE KERORO PLATOON IS COMING APART AT THE SEAMS.

LET'S HOPE YOUR ENEMIES DON'T GET WIND OF THIS...

ELSEWHERE IN TOKYO...

IN A REMOTE SHIPPING YARD...

HMM...
SO...THERE'S INTERNAL DISCORD AMONG THE KERONIAN DISPATCH UNIT.
YES, SIR. THIS IS YOUR CHANCE, SIR!!
No Ent

WOULD YOU TAKE CARE OF THEM, SIR?!!
THOSE GUYS HIT ME--TWICE!!
I'VE NEVER BEEN HIT--NOT EVEN BY A CUSTOMER!!

WHAT'S IN IT FOR ME?
DON'T WORRY--JAMA NET WILL TAKE CARE OF IT!!

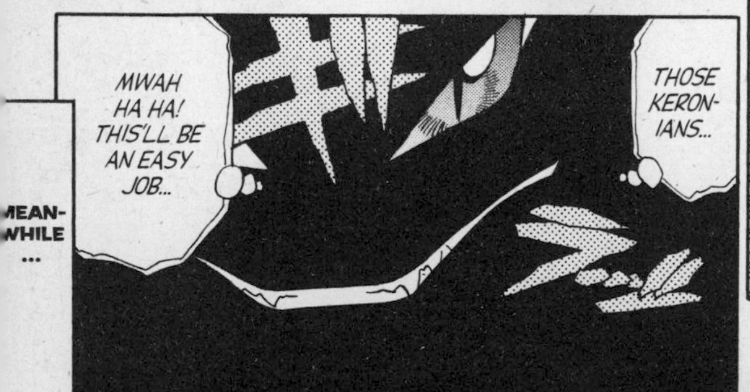
THOSE KERONIANS...
MWAH HA HA! THIS'LL BE AN EASY JOB...
MEANWHILE...

SHI-BUYA, TOKYO ...
THIEF! G-GIVE THAT BACK!
WHAT? Y'MEAN THIS?
NOT MOA-CHAN-- BUT ASAMI-CHAN!
G-GIVE IT BACK!!!
THAT MONEY IS FOR READING MY FAVORITE MANGA-- "LIEUTENANT TOAD"-- AND COLLECTIBLE STORAGE, AND BUYING DOMINOS, AND--!
SHUT UP, JERK!
?
!!!!?
KYAAA! WHAT THE--?!
WOOHOO! THANKS FOR THE NICE VIEW!
AND KEEP THE CASH! I'VE GOTTEN MY MONEY'S WORTH!
TMP

POKO-PENIANS HAVE SO MUCH TROUBLE AMONGST THEM-SELVES.
SHING
IT SEEMS PROTECTING THE EARTH IS NO EASY TASK.

YOU'RE TOO SERIOUS, DORORO.
I MEAN, YOU FINALLY MET UP WITH YOUR COMMRADES, ONLY TO BREAK OFF YOUR FRIEND-SHIP WITH THEM...

NO... IT WAS THE RIGHT THING TO DO.
AFTER ALL, I AM NOW ON THE SIDE OF EARTH.
SO ALL HER INVADERS--INCLUDING KERORO--ARE NOW MY ENEMIES!

I JUST FELL IN LOVE WITH THIS PLANET.
AND I MUST ALSO REPAY MY DEBT TO YOU, MASTER KOYUKI.
SEE? YOU ARE TOO SERIOUS!

!?

CORPORAL DORORO AND THE FEMALE NINJA KOYUKI-- HOW DID THEY MEET? WHAT HAPPENED BEFORE THEY MET UP WITH THE REST OF THE TROOP? THE STORY MUST BE TOLD ANOTHER TIME, SINCE AT THIS MOMENT...

WHO IS IT?!
HSSS, HSSS, HSSS... YOU SHOULD BE WORRIED ABOUT YOURSELVES, NOT EARTH!
I'VE FOUND YOU, KERONIAN!
Y-YOU ARE--!!!

DON'T YOU WANT A SNACK, SERGEANT?

......

WELL, FRIENDSHIPS ARE DIFFERENT FOR EVERYONE...

HE MUST BE WORRIED ABOUT HIS FRIEND.

PER-HAPS, YOUNG FUYUKI. BUT MORE LIKELY, HE'S JUST ASLEEP.
NNN...
NNN...
drool
WHA?!!

WHAT?! WHAT?! WHAT IS IT?! WHAT?!
WHAT?!
SERGEANT-- YOUR HEAD!!
THERE'S SOMETHING STUCK IN YOUR FORE-HEAD!!
A POST-CARD?
SHLIP
OOOF!

THAT IS ZERORO'S SPECIAL COMMUNICATION TECHNIQUE!!
WHAT DOES IT SAY?!

"DORORO HAS BEEN CAPTURED-- BY AN ALIEN CALLED VIPER OR SOMETHING!"
"I'M ASKING ALL HIS FRIENDS TO HELP HIM-- PLEASE!!!"
IT'S SIGNED, "KOYUKI."

VIPER?
WHAT DOES THIS MEAN, SARGE?
......

VIPER?!!
!?

WE MUST GO...
...RESCUE ZERORO!!

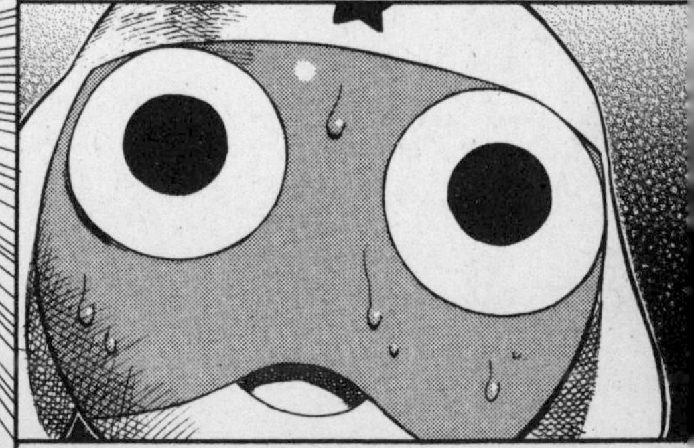

KERORO PLATOON EMERGENCY DEPLOYMENT !!!

ヒュウウウ...

LIKE A FROG BITTEN BY A SNAKE, DORORO IS COMPLETELY HELPLESS...
WHO ARE YOU, ANY-WAY?!

HSSS, HSSS, HSSS... YOU MIGHT SAY WE ARE THE KERONIANS' NATURAL ENEMIES!
SINCE THE BEGINNING OF TIME, WE'VE BEEN HUNTING THESE GULLIBLE IDIOTS!

I GUESS I'LL SELL YOU OFF TO A COSMIC MERCHANT.
FEMALE POKO-PENIANS SEEM TO FETCH HIGH PRICES, AMAZINGLY ENOUGH.
HOW DARE YOU?!

HOLD IT RIGHT THERE!!
!?
AHH... WITH THE POISON, YOU CAN'T EVEN TALK, CAN YOU?!
....

×3

VIPER!! WE WON'T LET YOU HAVE YOUR WAY WITH HIM!!
LET ZERORO GO!!

KERORO, TOO... MY EX-CAPTAIN?!
HSSS, HSSS, HSSS... SPEAKING OF GULLIBLE IDIOTS, LOOK WHO'S HERE!

FOOLS-SSS!!!
!!
NO EFFECT !!
TAKE THIS, YOU SNAKE !!!
TOO SSSSS-SLOW!!
SKREEE!
KU, KU, KU, KU ...
ROAR!
ACK!
CRACK

HA-HA-HISS! HA-MWAH HISS-HA!
ITHOUT THEIR MPLETE NITS, RONIANS ARE THING!!
KERORO PLATOON: COMPLETE DEFEAT?!

HOW CAN THIS BE...?!

IF...IF ONLY ALL FIVE OF US WERE TOGETHER...

I'M SORRY, ZERORO!

I AM REALLY, REALLY SORRY!!

ZEROROOO!!!

I'M SORRY... I'M THE ONE WHO BROKE YOUR PRECIOUS TAMAGORO...

IT WAS ME!!!

I JUST PUT IT IN MY POCKET TO BORROW FOR A LITTLE WHILE...

...AND I WAS GOING TO TELL YOU AND POLOGIZE, BUT... I JUST COULDN'T!!!

AND AT THAT MOMENT, A STRANGE SWITCH WENT OFF...

...IN KERORO'S STATE OF TRAUMA!

WE ARE...
FRIENDS ONCE MORE!!

WH...
...WHAT'S GOING ON?!
RESURRECTION!
THE KERORO PLATOON IS REASSEMBLED!!!
LET'S GO!!!
YO!!
KERORO PLATOON EXCLUSIVE SUPER SPECIAL WEAPON!!!
KERONICAL CRUSH CHASING CRYSTAL SLAM DUNK!!!
Energy Ball generated!!!
DOUBLE DRIBBLE !!
NICE SHOT!!
TRAVELING!!

WE'RE COUNTING ON YOU ...
... DORORO !!!
LIGHT WITH THE LEFT HAND... ALL IN THE WRIST...
WH-WHY CAN'T I MOVE ?!!
I MEAN...
...IT SEEMS AS THOUGH... I SHOULDN'T MOVE!

GUYAAHHH!
WE DID IT!!!
SEE THE FORCE OF KERORO PLATOON WHEN ALL FIVE OF US ARE TOGETHER!!
WE HAVE WON!!
CAPTAIN, SIR...
HA!
HA HA HA... ♪

HOW **NICE** FOR YOU, DORORO!

MASTER KOYUKI!!!

YOU MUST STAY FRIENDS...

...FROM NOW ON! ♪

SO, DORORO... I HEAR YOU ARE PROTECTING THE PEACE HERE ON EARTH!

THAT IS CORRECT.

WELL, IF WE INVADE IT...

...AND ALSO MAKE IT **PEACEFUL**, THEN THAT'S TWO BIRDS WITH ONE STONE, EH?!

WE MUST FIGHT TOGETHER!!

YES, WE SHA--

WHAT'S WRONG?

KERORO-KUN...YOU BROKE MY TAMAGORO.

YES, THAT'S RIGHT. SO?

I HAD SUCH A TERRIBLE TIME...

I WAS HARD ON MY **MOTHER**... I BLAMED MY **BROTHER**...

HUH?

HYAAAAAA?!

I must think on this awhile. -Dororo

MISTER SERGEANT, SIR- ANOTHER NOTE!!
Cough! Gag!
NOW WHAT'S GOING ON?!

SO THE FIFTH ONE TOOK OFF AGAIN AFTER ALL!
AH HA HA. WELL, AT LEAST IT'S PEACEFUL AGAIN!

KOYUKI-CHAN!!
NO! YOU'VE MOVED IN ACROSS THE STREET?!
NATSUMI-SAAAN!!

OF COURSE, NATSUMI HAD NO CLUE...
...THAT--HOWEVER PROVI-SIONALLY--THE KERORO PLATOON HAD RE-ASSEMBLED.
....
IT'S SO NICE THAT YOU'LL BE MY NEIGHBOR, NATSUMI-SAN! ♪
YEAH--I'M GLAD TOO! ♪
TO BE CONTINUED

ENCOUNTER LVII
EMERGENCY WARNING! KOYUKI AZUMAYA APPROACHING!!

DING DONG
I, JUNIOR HIGH STUDENT KOYUKI AMAZUYA...
...FELL IN LOVE AT FIRST SIGHT ON MY VERY FIRST DAY IN TOKYO!
COMING!
KOYUKI-CHAN! YOU CAME TO GET ME?
TEE-HEE! ♪
DO YOU MIND?
NOT AT ALL! IT'S REFRESHING-- THIS IS THE FIRST TIME SINCE GRADE SCHOOL!
SHE'S NICE, RELIABLE, AND CITY-LIKE...
...FAR BETTER THAN ANY OF THE MENFOLK ♡ I KNOW...
I'M OFF TO SCHOOL!
MASTER FUYUKI... WHO IS THAT FEMALE YOUTH?
THAT'S KOYUKI-SAN--SHE'S A CLASSMATE OF NATSUMI'S.
CTUALLY, SHE JUST MOVED INTO THE HOUSE BEHIND US.

?
HMM... HER FACE SEEMS SOMEHOW FAMILIAR.
BUT WHAT IS THIS UNCOMFORT-ABLE CURRENT THAT'S MAKING ME SHUDDER ...?

NOW, NOW, GIRORO-KUN!
SHE'S JUST A GIRL-FRIEND!
That woman is getting...
...too close to my Natsumi!
YOU GO ON TO SCHOOL TOO, MASTER FUYUKI!
O-KAY... JUST MAKE SURE YOU DON'T DO ANYTHING YOU'LL REGRET!

REALLY! YOUR LAST SCHOOL WAS TEN KILOMETERS AWAY?!
EH HEH HEH. WELL, I LIVED IN THE COUNTRY. ♪

OH--IT MUST'VE BEEN REALLY NICE.
MY GRANDMA LIVES WAY OUT IN THE BOONIES, TOO.

THE AIR AND WATER ARE SO NICE AND CLEAN THERE...
?

ざわ…
ざわ
?
?

KO-KOYUKI-CHAN? DON'T YOU THINK YOU'RE GETTING A LITTLE TOO CLOSE TO ME?!
I'M SORRY! I WAS JUST COLD! TEE-HEE! ♪
I MEAN, I DON'T MIND... BUT...

WILL YOU EAT LUNCH WITH ME?
S-SURE I WILL!

HEY!
WHO IS SHE?
All right!
TEXE

A TRANSFER STUDENT IS STEALING NATSUMI FROM US?!
I CAN'T STAND IT! SHOULD WE CONSIDER BULLYING HER INTO SUBMISSION?!

MEMBERS OF THE KISSHO SCHOOL WOMEN'S NATSUMI FAN CLUB

HEY... ISN'T IT KIND OF WARM HERE?
THAT'S WEIRD. THEY SAID IT WAS GONNA BE COLD TODAY.
IT'S NOT JUST WARM, BUT STRANGELY AND DISGUSTINGLY WARM...

UGH! IT'S SO GROSS!
HEY, CLASS IS ABOUT TO START-- LET'S GO!
YOU CAN'T FOOL ME!
THAT WOMAN IS DANGER-OUS!!!

NATSUMI-SAAAN! ♡
RRING

NATSUMI-SAN! ♡
NATSUMI-SAN! ♡
NATSUMI-SAAAN! ♡
Nat-sumi-saaan...
saaan...
saaan...
saaan...

I'M HOME!
ぐったり

WHAT'S WRONG, NATSUMI?
WELL, KOYUKI-CHAN...

..SHE'S A NICE GIRL AND EVERYTHING, SO I DON'T MIND, BUT...
...IT MADE ME SELF-CONSCIOUS OF OTHER PEOPLE WATCHING US, AND...

HUH. THEY TURN OFF THE LIGHTS REALLY EARLY NEXT DOOR.

WE ARE READY TO SUP.
THANK YOU, DORORO. ♪

THE DAY OF THE SHINOBI ENDS WITH A REPORT AT MEALTIME.

BON APPÉTIT!

I SHALL ENJOY THIS MEAL.

TODAY I GOT REALLY CLOSE TO NATSUMI-SAN!
CONGRAT-ULATIONS ARE IN ORDER.
YOU MUSTN'T TELL ANYONE THAT I'M A NINJA!
I DON'T WANT HER THINKING I'M WEIRD!
UNDER-STOOD!

I MUST ASK YOU, TOO, NOT TO DIVULGE MY PRESENCE HERE TO THE REST OF THE TROOPS.
OH? WHY?
すずず…

SINCE WE ONCE PARTED WAYS...
...I CANNOT RETURN TO THEM SO EASILY.
UNDER-STOOD!

BUT I MUST SAY, THESE CITY HOUSES JUST DON'T MAKE A HOME.
WITHOUT HIDDEN HALLWAYS AND SECRET STAIRS, IT'S SO INCON- VENIENT!
IN THAT CASE, YOU SHOULD ASK THE CAPTAIN...
はっ
NO, NO. NEVER MIND!
にゃあ~~
YOU'RE PRETTY STUB- BORN, DORORO!
WE FINALLY MOVED NEXT DOOR, BUT...
......
...ALTHOUGH ACTUALLY, THE MOVE WAS FOR ME, TOO... ♪
ほわん
ほわん
MAYBE I'LL GIVE HER ONE MORE PUSH...
TODAY... ♪
WELL, THEN!

IT'S SO WARMMM!

AND IT'S THE MIDDLE OF WINTER!

MANGA X

YOU SEE?

WE DON'T EVEN NEED HEATING!

GRUMBLE

HE'S BEEN LIKE THIS SINCE MORNING.

She is mine!

I CAN'T EVEN SEARCH FOR THE FIFTH ONE 'CAUSE OF IT!

SIR... YOU'VE BEEN SWALLOWED BY A PITCH-BLACK EMOTION.

WE ARE THE SAME, YOU AND I...MAYBE NOW WE CAN UNDERSTAND ONE ANOTHER...

I know. Natsumi the best!

I love all her quirks!

WHAT CAN WE DO ABOUT HIM?!

Ah ha ha!

HA HA HA....

FINALLY... I UNDER-STAND YOU, GIRORO, SIR.

MANGA X

ピンポーン

DING DONG

?

YES?
GOOD EVENING! ♪
OH, ER... AZUMAYA-SAN!

WHAT IS IT?
TEE-HEE!

WELL, SINCE WE JUST MOVED IN, WE CAN'T USE OUR BATH YET. SO...
I WONDERED IF I MIGHT USE YOURS.
OH! OF COURSE YOU CAN. COME ON IN!
THANK YOUUUUU! ♪

MY SISTER'S TAKING A BATH, THOUGH, SO YOU'LL HAVE TO WAIT...
?

HUH? AZUMAYA-SAN?
DON'T WORRY ABOUT ME!

SPLASH
SPLISH

ゆる ゆる
PHEEW. WARM AND NICE. IT FEELS SO GOOD.
EXCUSE ME...
That voice!
KYAAA! KO--KOYUKI-CHAN?!
I CAME TO WASH YOUR BACK! ♡
W-WELL... THAT'S REALLY NOT NECESSARY!
OH, NO-- I MUST!
THIS IS A NINJA-- I MEAN, A LOCAL TRADITION WHERE I COME FROM. ♪
COME, COME! DON'T BE SHY!
GAAHH!

Pheeew...
MISTER SERGEANT, SIR--DON'T YOU THINK IT'S A LITTLE HOT?
Gero... YES... PERHAPS THE HEATING SYSTEM IS ON TOO HIGH?
WHAT?!
OUR RED COMRADE IS... ALTHOUGH NOT WELL-EXPRESSED IN THIS MANGA...
...GETTING REDDER THAN EVER!!!
HYAAAAA!
OUCH!! HOT!! HOT!! OUCH!
HE'S DISAPPEARED...
HOW COULD HE HAVE?
THIS IS EMBARRASSING.
DON'T WORRY!
EVERYONE DOES THIS BACK IN THE OLD COUNTRY! ♡

WITH THAT FORM, YOU CAN'T EVEN TAKE ONE LAYER OF SKIN OFF!!
WATCH YOUR FORM!
SPLASH
KYA?!
GET AWAY!!!
I'LL SHOW YOU HOW IT'S DONE IN THE MILITARY!!!
!?
GET OUT!!

THAT WAS...
...DORORO'S OLD FRIEND, I THINK...

D-DID YOU SEE THAT? A BIG FROG--OR SOMETHING--CAME JUMPING IN!
DID YOU SEE IT, KOYUKI-CHAN?
UH, NOT REALLY... THE STEAM...
OH--GOOD! AH HA HA... ♪

HOW CAN YOU... AT A TIME LIKE THIS, WHEN THE FIFTH ONE IS ABOUT TO JOIN US...
WHAT WILL WE DO IF YOU KEEP GOING AROUND ACTING LIKE THAT?!
HAS NO MEMORY OF WHAT JUST TRANSPIRED.
Muu...

LETTING YOUR FEELINGS GET IN THE WAY OF OUR MISSION IS THE WORST THING YOU CAN DO!
Mu... Mmu... Mmmmuu...
TAKING THIS OPPORTUNITY TO THE MAX!

I'M SORRY, KERORO...

...I CAN'T BELIEVE IT...
...BUT... I MUST'VE LOST MY COOL.
GI-GIRORO?

AZUMAYA HOUSE: THE BACK DOOR ...

BANG
BANG
BANG
BOOM!
I SHOULD HAVE USED FORCE TO GAIN CONTROL TO BEGIN WITH!!
Giro Giro Giro Giro Giro Giro Giro Giro
NEVER REGAINED HIS COOL!
TRIP
!?
NNGH...?
A SECURITY TRAP?!

IN-
TRUDER
...
...NAME
THYSELF!
TMP
!!

GI-
GIRORO!
WHAT
BRINGS
YOU
HERE?!

DORORO...
WHY ARE
YOU
HERE?!
NEVER
MIND.
IT'S NOT
IMPORTANT
NOW.
Well, actually,
it is, but...

I'M HERE
FOR THE
FEMALE...
CLICK
OUT
OF THE
WAY!

DON'T
TELL
ANYBODY
THAT
I'M A
NINJA!

I'M SORRY--
BUT I CANNOT
LET YOU
PASS!
OH?
IS THAT
SO...?

I WILL PASS-- EVEN IF IT KILLS ME!
GIRORO VS. DORORO OUTBREAK!!

IT'S BEGUN...
KU, KU, KU, KU, KU...
BOOM
SHOOM
POW

Gero!
SO, HE WAS HIDING NEXT-DOOR ALL ALONG!
GIRORO'S STEPPED ON A LAND MINE, SO TO SPEAK!
KABLAM

ATTACK SOLDIER VS. ASSASSIN...
WHAT A SHOW!
KU, KU, KU, KU...

YOU MUST STOP THEM QUICK, MISTER SERGEANT, SIR!
Gero Ge--?!

YOU WANT ME TO GET IN THE MIDDLE OF THIS?
WE CAN'T AFFORD TO HAVE THE SUPERIOR OFFICER DIE... WHY DON'T YOU GO?
I DON'T WANT TO GO, EITHER!!
BLAM
BLAM
BLAM
BLAM
BLAM

I HATE TO DO THIS, BUT...
...YOU'LL HAVE TO DIE.
DORORO KILLING METHOD ...
METAMORPHOSIS DRAW DORORO SLASH!!!
CHINK
!?
FU, FU, FU...
DORORO ...
FOOOM
YOUR SIGNATURE MOVE IS USELESS! YOU CAN'T DEFEAT ME BY ATTACKING WITH THE BACK OF YOUR SWORD NOW!
HEY, DORORO'S FRIEND-- YOU'RE PRETTY GOOD!

じゃあん!
......!

BUT A NINJA'S DUEL NEEDS NO MEDDLING!
GO FOR IT, DORORO!

YOU! YOU'RE THE POKOPENIAN THAT WAS WITH DORORO BEFORE!
FU, FU, FU. YOU'RE NOT SO BAD, AFTER ALL.
TEE-HEE! HE HASN'T FIGURED IT OUT.

THIS IS THE WAY OF THE NINJA... HERE I GO!
ばっ
I'M READY, DORORO!!

BIFF
BAM
VOOM
KABOOM

POW
VAVOOM

WHY ARE ALL THOSE SCIENCE-FICTION TYPE SOUNDS COMING FROM NEXT DOOR?
NO. IT CAN'T BE...

PHEW! THOSE TWO ARE PRETTY GOOD!
THESE GUYS MAY JUST INVADE POKOPEN YET!
MISTER SERGEANT, SIR, THAT'S A HIGH-LEVEL PROBLEMATIC STATEMENT!!
WHAT ARE YOU WATCHING?
OH, ER... JUST PEEKING NEXT DOOR...

KYAAA-- MASTER NATSUMI ?!!
AND WHAT THE HELL IS GIRORO DOING THERE?!

WHAT DO YOU MEAN, GETTING THE NEIGHBORS INVOLVED LIKE THIS?!
BUT-- GIRORO DID THIS ON HIS OWN--
HYAAA! NO--OUCH, OUCH! I'M GOING TO CRY!

KOYUKI-CHAN!!
Kyaa!
...?

I THINK I'M LOSING SIGHT OF THE PURPOSE OF THIS BATTLE, BUT...
...IT'S TIME TO SETTLE THIS!!

WITH THE NEXT BLOW, ONE OF THEM WILL DIE...
WHAT?! NO WAY!

HERE I COME!!!

BOTH OF YOU, GO...
KYA!

OH, NO!
DUST IN MY EYE...

GIRORO !!!
WHAT DO YOU THINK YOU'RE DO--

NATSUMI-SAN...!
Oh, shoot ...
Nat-sumi ...?
KOYUKI-CHAN...?!

Gero Gero Gero Gero!
YOU WERE SO CLOSE TO US ALL THIS TIME!

WHY DIDN'T YOU TELL US?
I AM FILLED WITH SHAME.
YOU SURE MESSED THIS PLACE UP GOOD.

I SHALL REPAIR THIS AS YOU WISH WITH THE KERO BALL!
I AM INDEBTED TO YOU, CAPTAIN, SIR...
I'M GLAD FOR YOU, DORORO...

AS FOR ME, THOUGH...
...NATSUMI-SAN MUST HATE ME NOW.

DORORO WAS FOUND, AND GIRORO WAS TAKEN INTO CUSTODY...
BOX 'O GIRORO
THE NEXT DAY...

BON APPÉTIT.

I SHALL ENJOY THIS MEAL.

WOW. THIS PLACE FINALLY FEELS LIKE HOME!

AND ALL THIS THANKS TO YOUR FRIENDS, DORORO. ♪

DING DONG

I'M SORRY YOUR SECRET WAS REVEALED, MASTER KOYUKI...

NOT TO WORRY, DORORO. IT WASN'T YOUR FAULT!

KOYUKI-CHAAAN!
LET'S GO TO SCHOOL! ♫
NATSUMI-SAN!
MORNING, KOYUKI-CHAN!
UH... UMM...
IS IT OKAY?
I'M A LITTLE... STRANGE, YOU KNOW...
WHAT? THAT? NAHHH.
LET'S BE FRIENDS, OKAY? ♡
S-SURE!!
NATSUMI'S POWERS OF IMMUNITY ARE NOT JUST FOR SHOW!
COME ON IN!
OKAY...
KYAAA?!
NA-NATSUMI-SAN! THAT'S THE TRICK DOOR!
THIS IS THE FRONT DOOR!
TO BE CONTINUED

1. Dororo - The Fifth Member!
2. Petit Merger No. 17 - Doro-Head - Dororo
3. Sgt. Keroro
4. The images on this box are imaginary action diagrams of Petit Merging Alien No. 17
5. Corporal Dororo - No. 17 Doro-Head
6. If you combine Numbers 1 through 20, they become Mini Merging Robot Keroro Reb
7. Having fun with the joint pieces:
   - (1) Unlimited assembly and disassembly!
   - (2) All pieces fit!
   - (3) Make your own machine with different combinations!
   - (4) Combinations can only be done with Ao-hige plamodels! *
   - (5) If your budget is vast, promptly buy other available kits!

   * Plamodels (a combination of "plastic" and "models") are types of figurines!
8. Doro-Head Corporation, Inc., LTD.
   MADE IN JAPAN

ENCOUNTER LVIII
INVASION IN BLOOM!!
OPERATION: COSMIC FLOWER EXPO!

MOMMYYYY... I WANT THAT FLOWER!
I'M SORRY, HONEY. IT'S TOO HIGH!
BUT, MOMM-MMMYYY... I WANT IT!
....
POOF
WOW.
YEAH, YEAH!
THE FLOWER CAME TO ME!!
THAT'S NICE, DEAR.
CHINK

FORGIVE ME, FLOWER.
Gimme a break...
FOR EVERY ONE I CUT, I WILL PLANT TWO.
ONE FLOWER TO A LITTLE GIRL...
...MORE FLOWERS TO THE EARTH.
I WANT TO MAKE THIS BEAUTIFUL EARTH...
...MORE AND MORE BEAUTIFUL.
FOOOOOOOOOOOOO!!
WHAT--NO INFO YET?! DON'T TELL ME YOU'RE STILL IN CHRISTMAS MODE?!
...
YEAH--AND THE STUFF I ASKED FOR YESTERDAY, UH-HUH, WOULD YOU PLEASE, YAH-HUH, GET ON THAT, TOO?
RING
RING
YEAH, THAT'S IT! PUT A HOLD ON IT! YEAH--ABOUT 30 GALLONS?!
NO, NO-- DON'T SELL YET!
CAN'T MAKE IT ON TIME? IT'S YOUR JOB TO MAKE IT ON TIME!
THEN ADD SOME MORE SALT AND DILUTE IT MORE! THEY'LL NEVER KNOW THE DIFFERENCE-- DON'T WORRY, DON'T WORRY!!

HEY, YOU--
GIRORO! IF YOU'RE FREE, FIVE SHEETS OUTPUT!!
OKA--

KERORO... YOU'RE WORKING ...?
OF COURSE I AM!

WE'VE FINALLY FOUND THE FIFTH ONE!
OUR FUTURE IS NOW! OUR DREAMS HAVE ALMOST COME TRUE!!

IF I CAN JUST GENERATE A BUNCH OF INVASION PLANS LIKE THIS, I KNOW DORORO WILL COME AND JOIN US! I JUST KNOW IT!!
YES?! HELLO?!
Y-YOU'RE RIGHT! OF COURSE YOU'RE RIGHT!!

KERORO-- HOW ABOUT SOME COFFEE?!
PLEASE! AND LOTS OF SUGAR, SO IT'S CRAZY-SWEET!

YES, SIR!!!

KERORO IS WORKING...
SO LONG... IT HAS BEEN SO LONG... BUT FINALLY, OUR DAY IS HERE!
FU, FU... YES... FU, FU, FU, FU, FU!
FU, HA! FU, HA, HA, HA, HA, HA, HA!!

WHAT'S UP WITH HIM?
WEIRDO...
Giro Giro
Giro Giro
Giro Giro
Giro Giro
Giro Giro
Giro Giro

OKAY, DORORO!!
IF THERE'S A PLAN HERE THAT YOU LIKE...

...PLEASE FEEL FREE TO COME AND JOIN US!

....
VERY WELL.

YAHOOOOO!!
GOOD, GOOD! LET'S START WITH THIS ONE!!
スチャ

"OPERATION: SERIOUS SKIN DAMAGE! HOLEY MACKEREL OZONE HOLES, IRREVOCABLE BLUNDER"!!
WE'LL DESTRUCT THE OZONE WITH CFC BEAMS!! WE'LL DEFEAT THE POKOPENIANS UNDER MASSIVE AMOUNTS OF UV RAYS!
WELL--OKAY! I THOUGHT THAT ONE MIGHT BE A LITTLE TOO VIOLENT ANYWAY.
NEXT ONE-- NEXT!
SHINK
"OPERATION: SOLVE THE HAY FEVER PROBLEM!! IT'S THE LET ALL THE FORESTS BURN TO THE GROUND SHOW"!!
BLACK CLOUDS COVER POKOPEN! TEMPERATURES RISE HIGHER AND HIGHER AS A RESULT OF ACCUMULATING CO2!
?

HOT-CHA! HOT! HOT! HOT!
WHAT A THRILLING AND MOVING IMAGE!!
IT'S THE LET THE SERGEANT BURN TO THE GROUND SHOW!!
SHINK

UM...F-FIRE IS HARD TO HANDLE...SO MAYBE NOT THAT ONE!

BUT HOW ABOUT THIS?
WE'LL STREAM SOME GROUND-BREAKING, POPULAR CONTENTS ON BROADBAND!!
....
A CAMPAIGN TO TURN GASOLINE INTO COKE!
......!
THE BOB SAPP* DAM, BOB SAPP CANNON, AND BOB SAPP TANK...ALL WILL BE SECRETLY DEVELOPED SIMULTANEOUSLY! THE SO-CALLED "OPERATION: BS-III"!!
......!
IT'S BRILLIANT, RIGHT?
......
A PLAN TO TAKEOVER EARTH'S PERFORMING ARTS HIGH SCHOOLS!!
....

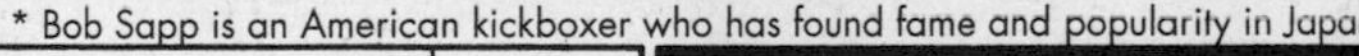
* Bob Sapp is an American kickboxer who has found fame and popularity in Japan

ALL REJECTED!

DORORO... YOU CAN'T JUST REJECT EVERYTHING!
YEAH! THE SERGEANT WORKED SO DESPERATELY TO COME UP WITH ALL THESE...FOR ONCE...

WHAT KIND OF PLAN DO YOU WANT, THEN?!
WHY DON'T YOU COME UP WITH SOMETHING YOURSELF?!

FLOWERS ....
I WANT TO FILL THIS TOWN WITH FLOWERS.
FLOWERS?!
UM, KERORO...
...WHY DID YOU AGREE TO SUCH A STUPID PLAN?!
FLOWERS HAVE NOTHING TO DO WITH INVADING POKOPEN!
WELL, IN THIS CASE A SPIRIT OF COOPERATION IS PARAMOUNT!
モグ モグ
WHAT A BUNCH OF--!
I CAN'T EAT FLOWERS ...
WHAT DO YOU THINK ABOUT THIS, LADY MOA?
WHAT'S YOUR HONEST OPINION ABOUT THIS OPERATION?
WELL... TO BE PERFECTLY FRANK...
...ALL THE OPERATIONS UNTIL NOW SEEMED TO BE MISSING SOMETHING.
I MEAN, IT WOULD'VE BEEN CRAZY TO THINK THAT THEY MIGHT HAVE WORKED...
...BUT... MOSTLY... IT'S BEEN TIRING JUST PUTTING UP WITH THEM. BUT PERSONALLY...

BEEP
BEEP
HELLO-- THIS IS "WINTER."
whisper
whisper
"WINTER" SPEAKING-- COME IN, PLEASE!
whisper
whisper
"SUMMER" HERE.
UH HUH... UH HUH....
TOWN FULL OF FLOWERS?
WHAT? WHAT DO YOU MEAN?
I DON'T KNOW... BUT THAT'S WHAT THEY SAID!
EARTH DEFENSE FORCE HEADQUARTERS (FOR BETTER OR WORSE)

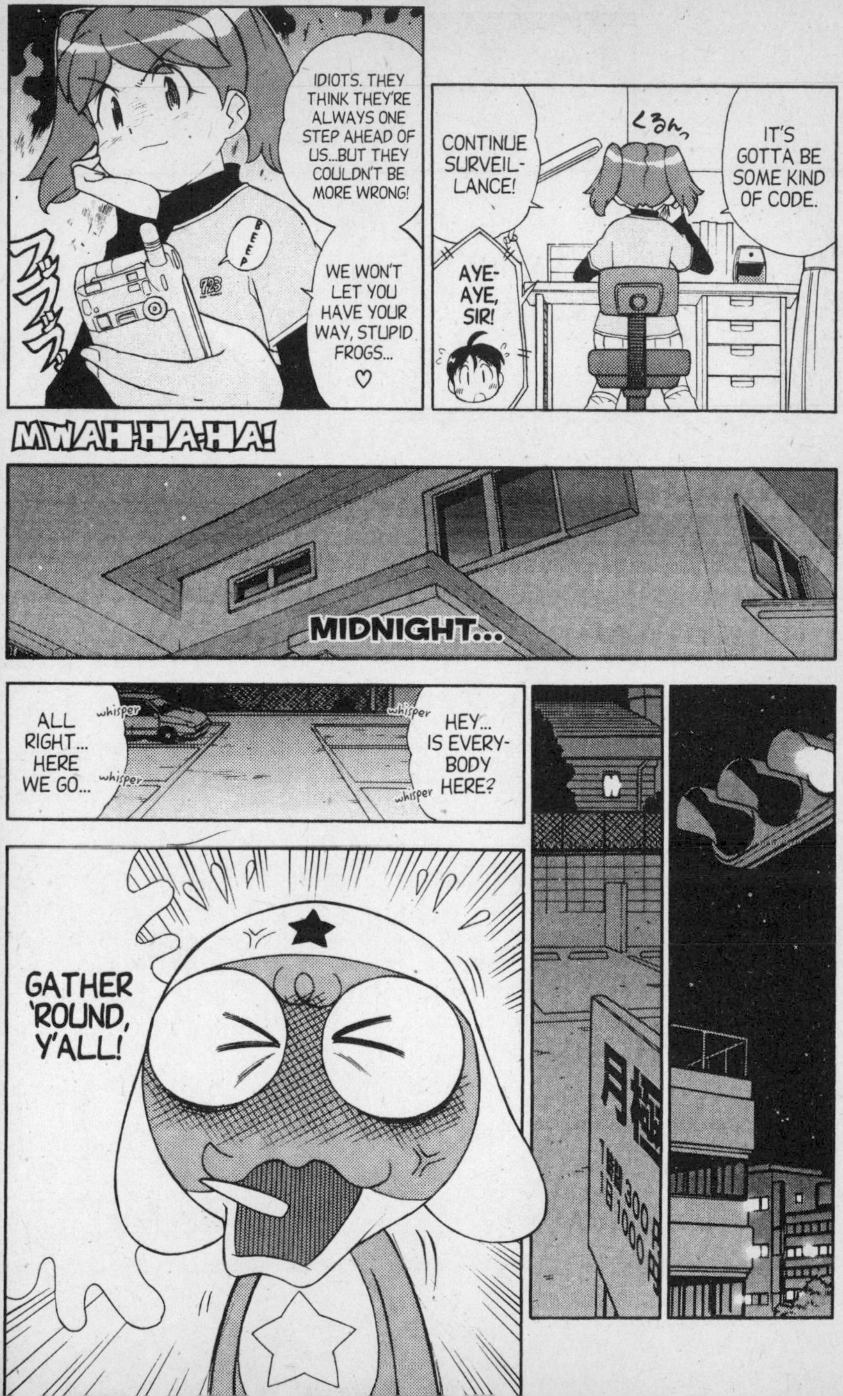

IT'S GOTTA BE SOME KIND OF CODE.
くるんっ
CONTINUE SURVEIL-LANCE!
AYE-AYE, SIR!

IDIOTS. THEY THINK THEY'RE ALWAYS ONE STEP AHEAD OF US...BUT THEY COULDN'T BE MORE WRONG!
BEEP
WE WON'T LET YOU HAVE YOUR WAY, STUPID FROGS... ♡

MWAH-HA-HA!

MIDNIGHT...

HEY... IS EVERY-BODY HERE?

whisper

whisper

ALL RIGHT... HERE WE GO...

whisper

whisper

GATHER 'ROUND, Y'ALL!

WE'RE ALREADY HERE! ♪

WHY ARE YO YELLI IDIOT

A WARRIOR CANNOT BE TOO CARE-FUL.

WHAT? LET'S GET STARTED ALREADY! ♪

TEH HEH HEH. SORRY...

UPON THIS MEMORABLE DAY, WE SHALL...

CUT THE CRAP AND GET ON WITH IT!

Hmph!

IF YOU PLEASE-- EACH OF YOU SHALL TAKE THESE "FLOWER SEEDS" AND SOW THEM AROUND THE BASE!

THEY HAVE BEEN GENETICALLY MODIFIED TO BLOSSOM ALL AT ONCE TOMORROW MORNING!

GOOOO TEAM!!
THIS POKOPENIAN TOWN WILL SOON BE FILLED WITH OUR FLOWERS...
...HENCE, A SHINING VICTORY FOR US!!
NO SUB-STANCE... BUT IT WILL HAVE SYMBOLIC MEANING.
PERHAPS IT'S NOT SO BAD TO HAVE OPERATIONS LIKE THIS ONCE IN A WHILE.
おお―!!

ばばーっ
COMMENCE OPERATION !!
DEPLOY !!!
I LOVE THIS KIND OF MIS-CHIEF!
BAH! IDIOTIC.
YEAH-- I GET TO PLAY ALL NIGHT!
I'M SLEEPY, BUT I'LL DO MY BEST!
WE'LL TAKE THE HIGH AREAS. ♡

I'M DOING IT, TOO! WHEE!

I DUNNO... LOOKS LIKE THEY'RE JUST HAVING FUN, SIS...
IDIOT! DON'T BE FOOLED.

Awoooo...
オオ〜…
オォン
オォン

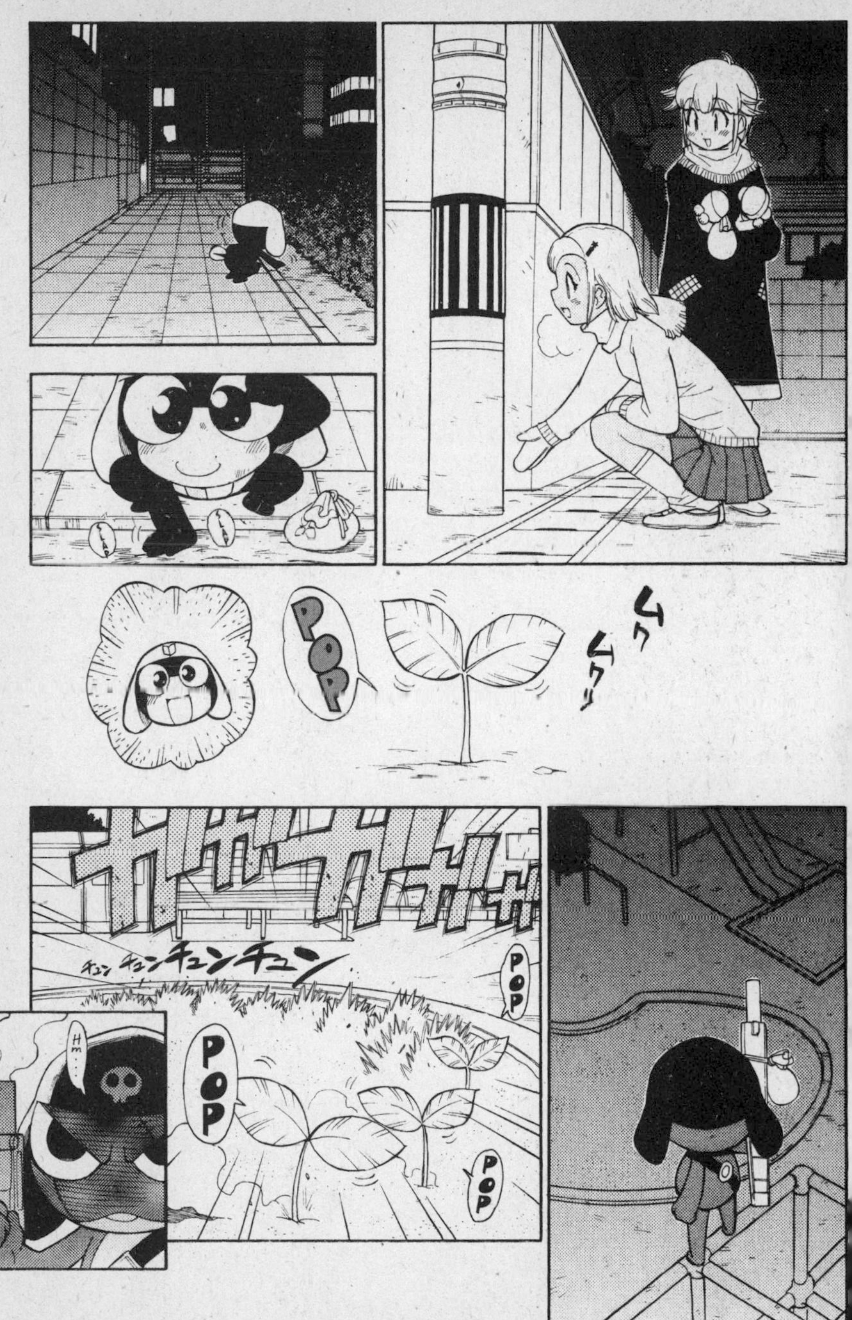

SLAP
SLAP
ムク
ムクリ
POP
チュン チュン チュン チュン
POP
POP
POP
Hm...

THERE YA GO!

HEH HEH HEH... WELL DONE! ♪

THEY DON'T LOOK LIKE THEY'RE DOING ANYTHING BAD...
FUYUKI! I TOLD YOU NOT TO BE FOOLED BY THEM!!

POP
POP
POP

POP

TO BE HONEST, I WASN'T SURE ABOUT THIS OPER-ATION...
...BUT PLANTING SEEDS LIKE THIS, THINGS REALLY TAKE ON A NEW MEANING!

THEY COULD BE MAN-EATING PLANTS ...
...plant a seed for my old man...
!!

THERE'S BEEN SO MUCH BAD NEWS AND HORRIBLE HAPPENINGS ON POKOPEN THESE DAYS...
AS A SENIOR COSMIC FELLOW, THIS WILL BE MY CONTRIBUTION TO POKOPEN'S WELL-BEING.
....

I CAN JUST IMAGINE THE EXPRESSIONS ON THE POKOPEN-IANS' FACES THIS MORNING WHEN THEY SEE THESE FLOWERS!
THEY'LL BE SURPRISED AT FIRST--BUT THEN THE EXPRESSION WILL CHANGE TO: "I'LL GIVE IT MY BEST AGAIN TODAY..."
I'M GOING TO LOVE SAYING, "HEY, I DID THAT!" I JUST CAN'T WAIT! ♪

SERGEANT !!
I WANT TO HELP, TOO!
MASTER FUYUKI!!
IN THAT CASE, YOU CAN TAKE OVER THIS AREA!
GOT IT!
じた
YOU... FUYUKI ...!
じた
OPERATION COMPLETE !!
WITHDRAW TROOPS!!
GOOD WORK, MEN!!

YOU'RE LATE, KERORO!
GOOD MORNING, UNCLE! ♡
Yawn! 'MORNING.

GOOD MORNING! ♬
YAWN!

WE ARE COMING UP ON OUR SCHEDULED BLOSSOM DETONATION TIME...
...WHEN BLOOMING COMMENCES, IT WILL ALL SHOW UP ON THIS MONITOR.

COM-MENCING COUNT-DOWN!
3...
2...
1...

Flower map

STATION

WE DID IT!

TOTAL SUCCESS!!!

LOOK, LOOK!
I PLANTED THESE ONES HERE!!
WHAT ...?!
THE FLOWER SYMBOLS ARE DIS-APPEARING...
VOOM
VOOM
VOOM
WH-WHAT'S HA-HAPPENING ?!!
LET'S GO SEE, SER-GEANT !!
HANG TIGHT, MEN! I MUST ASSESS THE SITUA-TION!!
....

HERE, TOO...
AND OVER THERE!
THEY'RE ALL GONE...
WHAT IS THE MEANING OF THIS?
ALL RIGHT.
ALL RIGHT.

THIS IS THE LAST OF THEM.
OKAY, ON TO THE NEXT SPOT. C'MON!
BUT...
...THOSE ARE...

EX-EXCUSE ME! WAIT A MINUTE!!
あっ
WHY ARE YOU TAKING THE FLOWERS?!

WELL, SON, IT'S A REAL NUISANCE WHEN SOMEONE DOES THIS WITHOUT A PERMIT...
WE ALL HAD TO WORK ON OUR DAY OFF!
DON'T YOU KIDS EVER DO ANYTHING LIKE THIS!
WAIT A MINUTE!
Y-YOU DON'T HAVE TO THROW THEM ALL AWAY...
CAN'T YOU LEAVE JUST A FEW BEHIND?!
N-NATSUMI
SOMEONE TOOK HIS TIME TO PLANT THESE, YOU KNOW!
MASTER NATSUMI...
I-I HAVE NO AUTHORITY TO DO ANYTHING...
GRAB

Ho ho ho!
PAUL-SAN!!
MIS-TRESS MO-MOKA!
Good morning.
MAY I SPEAK TO YOU FOR A MOMENT?
WH-WHAT...? WHAT?!
ABOUT THAT LOAD...
...THERE ON YOUR TRUCK...
NISHIZAWA GROUP WOULD LIKE TO PURCHASE IT.
DON'T WORRY, WE'VE ALREADY SPOKEN TO THE CITY...
Just write in any amount you please here...
I... I don't know...
NISHIZAWA-SAN!
THANK GOODNESS I GOT HERE IN TIME!
THANK YOU, MOMOKA-CHAN!!!
I WILL PLANT ALL OF THESE FLOWERS ON AN ISLAND OWNED BY NISHIZAWA GROUP!
WE CAN'T LET ALL THESE FLOWERS GO TO WASTE! ♡

YAHOO! I'M SO GLAD!!

I GUESS I COULD CALL THIS A SEMI-SUCCESS...

I GRABBED ONE LAST FLOWER AS A MEMENTO.
I GOTTA ADMIT, IT'S PRETTY NICE FOR SOMETHING **THEY** CAME UP WITH...

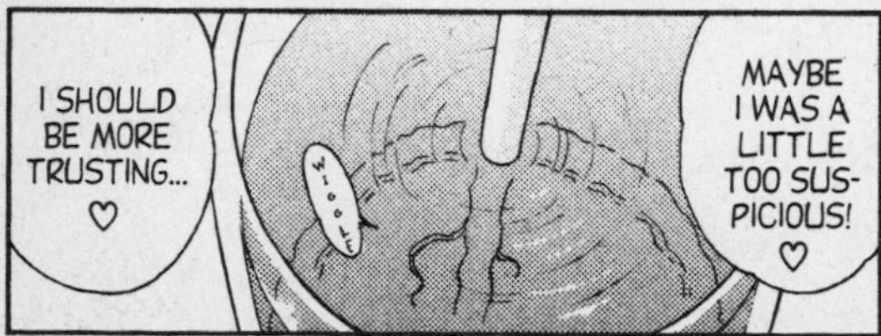
MAYBE I WAS A LITTLE TOO SUS-PICIOUS! ♡
I SHOULD BE MORE TRUSTING... ♡
WIGGLE

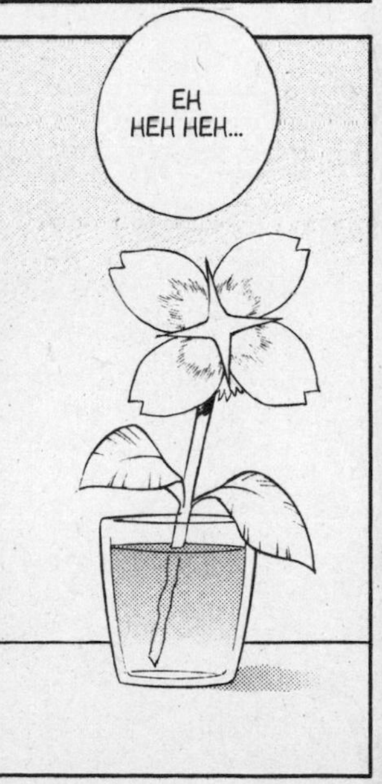
EH HEH HEH...

THANK YOU...
...FOR GOING ALONG WITH MY PLAN.

SAY NO MORE!
I'M JUST GLAD WE WERE FINALLY ABLE TO DO SOMETHING TOGETHER-- AS A TEAM!!
CAPTAIN, SIR...

I, TOO...
...DIDN'T MIND THIS OPERATION SO MUCH.
GIRORO-KUN...

KYAAAAAA!!

KERON FORCE'S CUSTOM VEGETATION "COSMIC FLOWER EXPO I" (MANUFACTURED IN KULULU'S LAB) WAS LATER CONFIRMED TO HAVE SERIOUS DEFECTS IN GROWTH HORMONE REGULATORY FUNCTIONS.
HEELLPPP...
...MEEEEEE!
NO DOUBT THERE WILL BE OUTCRIES FOR A THOROUGH INVESTIGATION AS TO WHETHER THIS WAS INTENTIONAL.
NATSUMI?!

AT ABOUT THE SAME TIME, SOMEWHERE IN THE PACIFIC... A "MOVING ISLAND" WAS OBSERVED.
Oh!
IT WAS INSTANTLY DECREED THE OFFICIAL EIGHTH WONDER OF THE WORLD...
TO BE CONTINUED

SPRING...
...THE SEASON FOR NEW BEGINNINGS, BE IT A NEW SCHOOL OR A NEW JOB!

Note: In Japan, the school year begins in April. New college grads begin new jobs in April, as well.

ENCOUNTER LIX SPECIAL EFFECTS: JOB HUNTING MADE SIMPLE!!

AND...

...YOUR SPECIAL TALENTS, IT SAYS HERE, ARE...

鈴木探偵事務所
03-456
7890

Suzuki Private Investigation Office

..."NOT STOPPING IN THE MIDDLE OF THE STREET"? "NOT GIVING UP ON A DREAM"?

AND... "ADHESION"? WHAT'S THAT?

DOOOHH!!
UHYAAAA?!
THAT'S EASY!!
I'LL SHOW YOU!!
ADHE--
WHOA! STOP! STOP IT!!
I'M AFRAID YOU'LL HAVE TO TRY ELSEWHERE.
Suzuki, P.I.
WHINE WHINE
RUFF
WHINE
GREETINGS, YOUNG MONGEREL! I AM FREELANCE COSMIC DETECTIVE KOGORO (556)!
Bwa ha ha ha!
A ASSIONATE MAN WHO FOLLOWED HIS CHILDHOOD FRIEND, KERORO, TO EARTH!!
Don't make uch a sorry face!

NOWWWWW...
WHAT SHOULD WE HAVE FOR DINNER TONIGHT? ♪
OF COURSE--FISH! THEY SAY IT'S BRAIN FOOD, AFTER ALL.
THIS ONE FOR ME AND FUYUKI...
...AND THIS IS GOOD ENOUGH FOR THOSE IDIOTS. ♪
COME TRY IT!
IT'S DELICIOUS!
THAT PERSON IS...
REALLY DELICIOUS!
COME AND TRY!

HI! YOU'RE RABBIE-SAN, RIGHT?
OH! YOU'RE MY BROTHER'S FRIEND!
WOULD YOU LIKE TO TRY ONE?
UM... SURE!
DO YOU WORK HERE?
YES! WE NEED MONEY TO LIVE ON...
HEH?
MY BROTHER AND I HAVE BEEN LIVING HERE ON EARTH SINCE WE SAW YOU, BUT...
...PRICES ARE HIGH, AND THE JOB MARKET IS SO TIGHT... POKOPEN REALLY IS A DIFFICULT PLACE TO LIVE!
UH HUH....
Her second Pocky stick!
HER NAME IS RABBIE!
UPPORTING HER BROTHER, SHE IS TRULY A EMARKABLE LITTLE SISTER!

ALIENS HAVE IT SO HARD.

I THOUGHT THOSE ULTRA-MAN AND GODMAN TYPES KINDA LIVED AS THEY PLEASED...

...BUT I GUESS IT DEPENDS ON WHAT KIND OF ALIEN YOU ARE.

ON THE OTHER HAND...

Shake yer tush! Shake yer tush!

Wah ha ha ha!

I GUESS NOT ALL ALIENS BUM FOOD AND LODGING OFF HARDWORKING EARTH CITIZENS.

....
SHAKE YER TUSH! ♪ SHAKE YER TUSH! ♪
WHY IS SHE PRETENDING TO TALK TO NO ONE, WHEN IT'S CLEARLY DIRECTED AT A PARTICULAR PERSON? WHY DOES SHE DO THAT? ♪
STOP THAT. WHEN YOU DO IT, IT MAKES ME SICK.

IT AIN'T ALL PRETTY ON EARTH, WHAT WITH THE BAD ECONOMY AND SOARING UNEMPLOYMENT!
YOUR HIGHNESS--THAT'S MUCH TOO CRUEL!!!
YOU CAN GO BACK TO YOUR OWN PLANET ANYTIME YOU WANT, YOU KNOW.
OKAY, THEN. I'M INCREASING YOUR WORK QUOTA.
ANYTHING YOU SAY, MISTRESS.
NATSUMI'S REALLY GOOD AT PUTTING ON THE SQUEEZE FROM TIME TO TIME.

YES, THE RECESSION WAS STRONGLY AFFECTING ALIEN LIFE FORMS, TOO.
DUE TO FINANCIAL HARDSHIP, INVADERS--EVEN HEROES--WERE LEAVING EARTH LEFT AND RIGHT.
THE KERONIAN "BUBBLE ERA" WAS SO NICE. THEY SOLD SO MANY FUSA FUSA.*
CLONK
CLONK
CLONK

Motana Apartments

PHEEW ...
OKAY!
I'M HOME, BIG BROTHER!!

* An alien from planet Fusa Fusa, which means "lots of hair" in Japanese.

HA HA HA HA! WELCOME HOME, RABBIE!!
I'M GLAD YOU'RE SAFE AND SOUND! HA HA HA HA!
I HAVE SOME-THING GOOD TO REPORT TODAY!!
REALLY? YOU FOUND A JOB?
NO-- LOOK!! THIS PLASTIC BOX!
IF YOU TURN IT AROUND, YOU CAN USE IT AS A DESK!
....
AND I THINK THERE ARE OTHER WAYS YOU CAN USE IT, TOO!
Ha ha ha ha!
OH...YOU DIDN'T FIND A JOB, THEN...?
WELL, I'M SURE IT COULDN'T BE HELPED. THEY SAY THERE'S A RECESSION ON POKOPEN!
IT'S NOT YOUR FAULT, KOGORO!
RABBIE...
YOU'RE SUCH A TALENTED COSMIC DETECTIVE...
I JUST KNOW YOU'LL FIND A GOOD JOB!!

LOOK! THEY GAVE ME BREAD CRUSTS AND BACON ENDS 'N' PIECES!

LET'S FEAST ON THESE AND GET HAPPY!!

AH...

NUH-UH!!

Ha ha ha ha...

ABOUT THE SAME TIME, AT KERORO PLATOON'S UNDERGROUND BASE...

KULULU'S LAB

...A NEW POKOPEN INVASION PLAN WAS BEING DEVISED!

PHEWW!

IT'S SO HARD ON MY BACK!

THAT BLASTED GIRL IS WORKING ME TO DEATH... USING THE RECESSION AS AN EXCUSE!

Ouch...

YO, KULULU... IS THAT THING PROGRESSING?

KU, KU, KU, KU...

IT'S FINISHED!!

WHOA!! THE GREAT KULULU DOES IT AGAIN!!

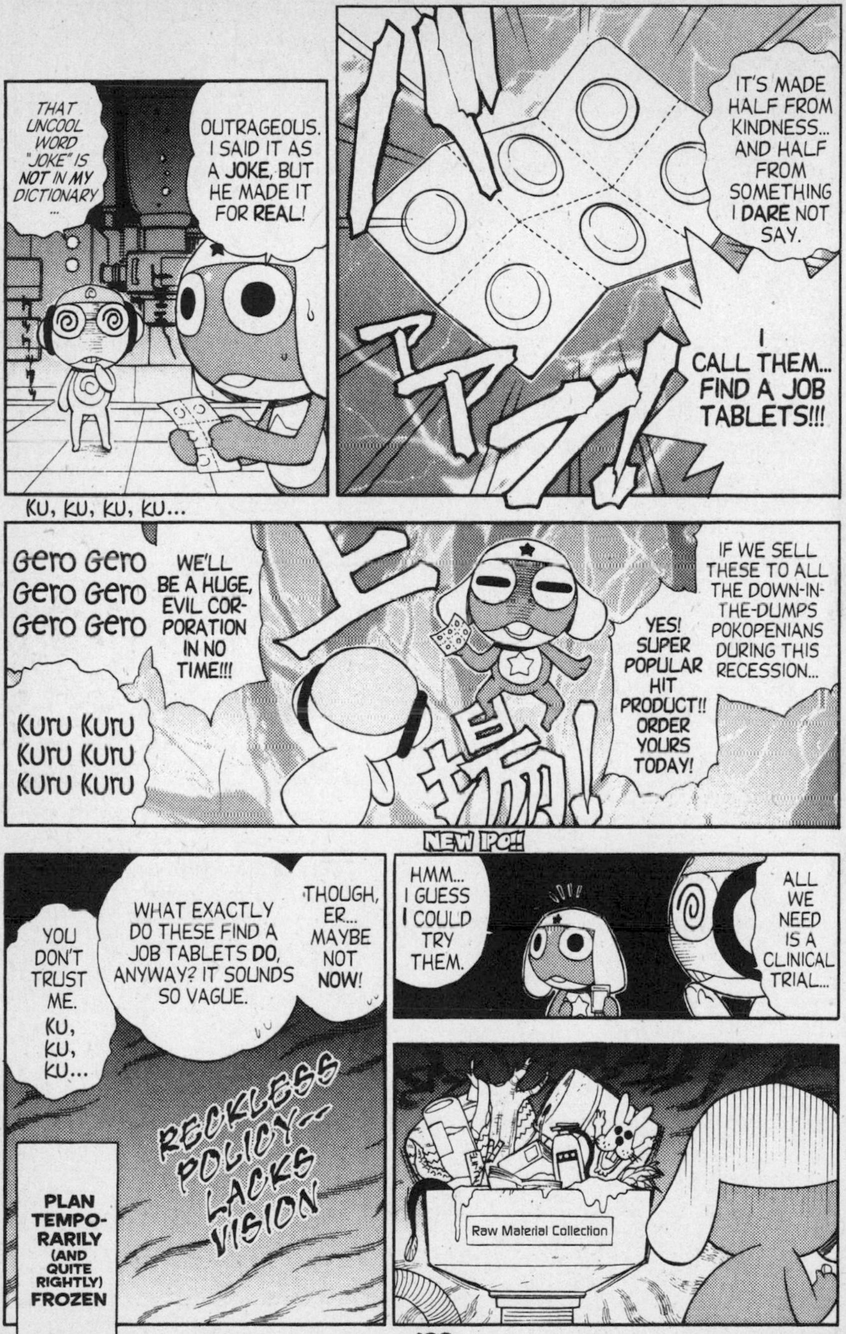

IT'S MADE HALF FROM KINDNESS... AND HALF FROM SOMETHING I DARE NOT SAY.
I CALL THEM... FIND A JOB TABLETS!!!
OUTRAGEOUS. I SAID IT AS A JOKE, BUT HE MADE IT FOR REAL!
THAT UNCOOL WORD "JOKE" IS NOT IN MY DICTIONARY...
KU, KU, KU, KU...
IF WE SELL THESE TO ALL THE DOWN-IN-THE-DUMPS POKOPENIANS DURING THIS RECESSION...
YES! SUPER POPULAR HIT PRODUCT!! ORDER YOURS TODAY!
WE'LL BE A HUGE, EVIL CORPORATION IN NO TIME!!!
Gero Gero Gero Gero Gero Gero
Kuru Kuru Kuru Kuru Kuru Kuru
NEW IPO!!

SEV-ERAL DAYS LATER...

HOW DID IT GO, BIG BROTHER?

OH...I SEE. YOU DIDN'T GET IT AGAIN.

Ha ha ha ha ha ha ha!

DON'T LOOK SO SAD, KOGORO...
WE'LL EXPLAIN! RABBIE HAS A SPECIAL ABILITY TO DECIPHER KOGORO'S EXPRES-SIONS!
IF ONLY THERE WERE SOMEONE WE COULD GO TO ON POKOPEN ...
.....!

Ha ha ha ha!

KOGORO!! I'VE GOT IT!!

HEY-- THAT IS A GREAT IDEA, RABBIE!!

OH, KOGORO! I HAVEN'T EVEN SAID ANYTHING, YET!

ME?
AS ONE WHO HAS HAD EXTENSIVE EXPERIENCE LIVING ON POKOPEN ?!

YES! WE NEED YOUR EXPERT ADVICE!
YEAH-- **YOUR** ADVICE, KERORO!!
Expert... Expert...
Extensive experience... Extensive experience...
CAN I ASK AGAIN? EXPERT?
YES, PLEASE-- AS AN EXPERT!!
MUA HA HA HA! VERY WELL, THEN!! I SHALL ADVISE!!
I WILL LISTEN TO WHAT YOU HAVE TO SAY!!
Unbelievable idiot...
UMM... THIS-- OOH! MY VOICE SOUNDS FUNNY!
TWO-WAY MIRROR
NOW WE CAN TALK WITHOUT WORRIES!!
VOICE-ALTERING MICROPHONE
WELL...WE'RE IN TROUBLE, BECAUSE KOGORO CAN'T GET ANY WORK...
I SEE. THEY SAY IT'S LIKE THAT EVERYWHERE THESE DAYS...
I see, I see...
BUT DOES HE **REALLY** WANT TO WORK?
OH, HE DOES! I THINK!

WHAT ABOUT SPECIAL SKILLS? DOES HE DRIVE A TRUCK OR ANYTHING?
WELLLLL...
YOU CAN DO ANYTHING IF THERE'S A BRIGHT, SUNNY SPOT AND AN UNENDING DREAM WITHIN YOU!
ばっ
HE SAYS, "NO."
HMM...TO BE HONEST, THIS MIGHT BE DIFFICULT.
YOU MIGHT WANT TO CONSIDER GOING BACK TO YOUR HOME PLANET.
WE'VE TRIED REALLY HARD ON OTHER PLANETS ALREADY, BUT NOTHING EVER WORKED OUT...
AND WE MADE A PACT... TO MAKE IT THIS TIME... ON POKOPEN!
B... BUT...!
sad music
WE PROMISED TO TRY HARD TOGETHER... JUST THE TWO OF US!
HEY...
パラパ～
THIS IS GETTING SO TOUCHING ...
パラ
UH-HUH...
WELL, TO BE QUITE HONEST, I CAN'T--
CAP-TAIN...
I BELIEVE WE MAY HAVE JUST THE THING.
KU, KU, KU, KU, KU...
!!!

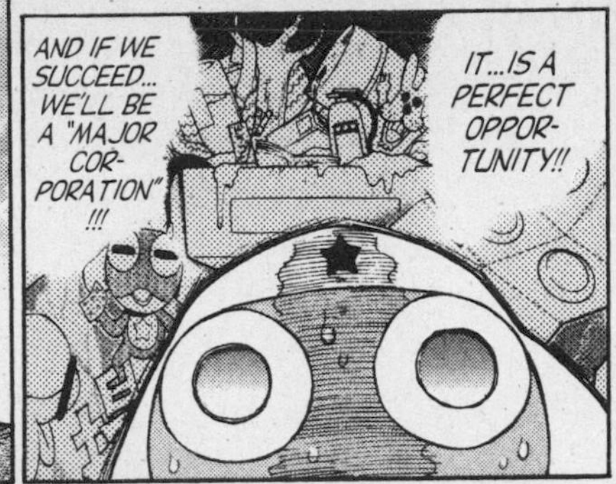
IT...IS A PERFECT OPPORTUNITY!!
AND IF WE SUCCEED... WE'LL BE A "MAJOR CORPORATION"!!!

?
BUT... I CAN'T LET A FRIEND... A FRIEND...
...A FRIEND TAKE SUCH A RISK!!

I HAVE THESE GREAT PILLS THAT MIGHT HELP... YOU WANT ONE?
REALLY ?!
ALL RIGHT!! THAT'S EXACTLY WHAT I WANT, KERORO!!
GULP

......
AND... HOW IS IT, 556?
NO STOMACHACHE... OR ANYTHING...?
HOW EXACTLY DOES ONE GET A JOB WITH THIS PILL?
BEATS ME... I HAVE NO IDEA WHAT HAPPENS FROM HERE.
MAYBE A RECRUITING AGENT WILL SUDDENLY JUMP IN FROM NOWHERE?
AH-HA HA-HA. GOOD ONE, MISTER SERGEANT, SIR!!

DID SOMEONE JUST COME INTO OUR HOUSE?
?

I'VE BEEN LOOKING FOR A CANDIDATE LIKE YOU!!
はっはっ?
PLEASE-- WON'T YOU COME WITH ME?!
はっはっ

YOU MEAN... IS THIS FOR A JOB?
OF COURSE IT IS!!

Ha ha ha ha ha ha ha!
WOW-- YOU DID IT, KOGORO!!
HA HA HA HA HA?!
COME-- HURRY, HURRY!!

AMAZINGLY EFFECTIVE...
......
Awestruck!
SLAM!

I MUST FOLLOW THEM!!
ME, TOO!!
I SHALL BE A WITNESS...
...TO HOW HARD YOU WORK, 556!!
SUCCESS ...
I STILL HAVE A LOT OF QUESTIONS...

WHAT ARE WE GOING TO DO WITHOUT OUR MAIN CHARACTER?

小泉演映撮影所

WE HAVE TO BROADCAST THE EPISODE THIS WEEK!

BUT THERE'S NOTHING WE CAN DO WITHOUT HIM!

WE ABSOLUTELY CANNOT HAVE A HOLE IN OUR BROADCAST!!

DIRECTOR!! WE CAN MAKE IT WORK!!

I FOUND A STAND-IN!!

Koizumitou Film Studio

HMM...HE DOES LOOK LIKE THE MAIN CHARACTER, KENJI KOBA-KUN. BUT...
...THE KEY TO THE SERIES WE'RE SHOOTING NOW, *COSMIC DETECTIVE GYOBON*, IS THE MAIN CHARACTER'S ABILITY FOR ACTION.
IF HE CAN'T DO ACTION...
ぶん!
ぶん!
I'M ROOTING FOR YOU, KOGORO ...
YOU MUST PROMOTE YOURSELF WELL!!
DO-OOH!!!
!!
ONE YEN...

IT!!!
I--
GOT--
HACK!
GRIN
IN ORDER TO PICK UP A ONE-YEN COIN, KOGORO SPENT 3,000 CALORIES (WHICH IS ANALOGOUS TO APPROXIMATELY 1,000 YEN)!!
HE'S IT!
HIS ACTION IS AT LEAST AS GOOD AS KOBA-KUN'S!
RIGHT!! YOU'RE HIRED!! GET READY TO SHOOT!!!
THIS IS GOING TO BE GREAT!!!
OKAY !!!
KOGORO, YOU DID IT!
YOU'VE FINALLY FOUND A JOB!!

I'M SO HAPPY FOR YOU...
...556!

YOU'VE FOUND YOUR DREAM JOB.
OKAY, SCENE 36!
ACTION !!!

AT LAST YOU'RE A REAL... COSMIC DETECTIVE...
EVEN IF IT IS JUST AN EFFECT OF THE MEDICINE...

RIGHT NOW... YOU'RE SHINING SO BRIGHTLY!
HEY, 556!

SO DIFFERENT FROM ME... WHO IS STILL WORKING UNDER A COMMONER...
FLAME OF JEALOUSY!
!?

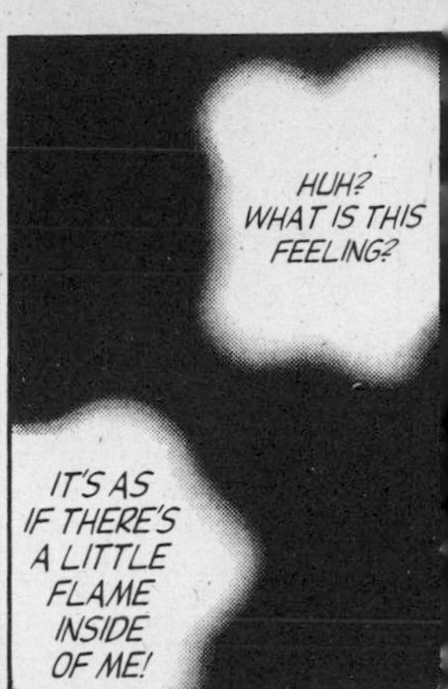
HUH? WHAT IS THIS FEELING?
IT'S AS IF THERE'S A LITTLE FLAME INSIDE OF ME!

I WANT TO BE HAPPY FOR MY FRIEND... AND YET...
...THIS UNEXPLAINABLE FEELING IN BATTLE-SHIP GREY...

HOW NICE!
WHY NOT ME?!
WHY NOT ME?!

IT'S NOT FAIR THAT ONLY 556-SAN GETS TO DO IT! I WANT TO DO IT, TOO!
TA-MAMA?!

GOOD! GOOD! GOOD!

HIS MOVEMENTS ARE HARDLY THAT OF AN AMATEUR!
TAKE THIS! AND THAT!
HE'S NO ORDINARY STAND-IN--HE'S A STAR!

I'M HERE TO HELP!!!

?

!!?

?

Aye Aye A-chooooh!

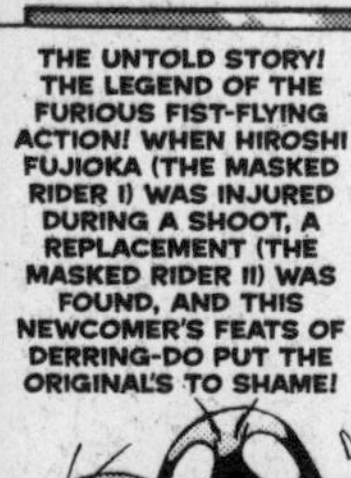

THE CAMERA!!

KOGORO'S WORKPLACE IS BEING DESTROYED!

PLEASE DO SOMETHING, KERORO-SAN!!

TAMAMA, YOU FOOL!

I AM... I AM...

...THE STRONGEST ONE THERE IS!!!

LET ME PLAY, TOO!!

GRAAAAAH!

UGYAAAAA!!

I'M HERE TO HELP, TOO, 556!!

KERORO... THIS IS SO REASSURING!!

TWO GREAT HEROES CO-STAR: THE DREAM OF A LIFETIME!! (NOTE SARCASM)

D-DIRECTOR!!

NO...NOT YET!! LET'S SEE WHAT HAPPENS!!

WHAT HAPPENS...?
The set --!!!
The man --?!!
THE GUN-POWDER STORAGE !!!
KOGORO'S...
...JOB...
OH...
OH...
sweaty palms
........!!
!?
PLEASE!! STOP IT... NOW!!!

IF YOU GET IN THE WAY OF KOGORO'S JOB...

...I WILL SHOOT!!

RABBIE?!

UH...

Y-YOU...

A SAD-EYED BEAUTY WITH A GUN...

THIS IS IT!! THIS IS THE EXACT IMAGE I WAS LOOKING FOR!!

YOU'RE **WONDERFUL!!!** WON'T YOU MAKE A PICTURE WITH ME?!

YOU! YOU ARE THE ONE I'VE BEEN LOOKING FOR!!

HUH?

ALL OF YOU CAN GO HOME NOW!
?
...
OH-- AND NEVER COME BACK!
556: UNEMPLOYED AGAIN!

HEY, SIS-- *GYOBON* IS ABOUT TO START!
ALL RIGHT, ALREADY. I'M COMING, I'M COMING!

IT'S A SPECIAL EPISODE TODAY.
HMM. THIS IS DIFFERENT FROM THE COMMERCIAL. I WONDER WHAT THEY'RE GOING TO DO?
!!

HEY? THAT--
ISN'T THAT RABBIE-SAN?
WITH THIS BROADCAST...
...RABBIE GOT HER HUGE BREAK AS THE "SAD-EYED GIRL WITH THE MACHINE GUN!"

AFTER THAT, LIFE FOR THIS BRAVE BROTHER AND SISTER TEAM WAS ...

LOOK, RABBIE!! IT CAN BE A BED, TOO!!
OH...I'M SO GLAD FOR YOU, KOGORO !!

はっはっはっは、
Ha ha hah ha!
STAY TUNED FOR THE NEXT EPISODE OF SGT. FROG!!

ENCOUNTER LX
A SPREADING CONTAGION?! RUNAWAY MAY DISEASE!

MAY...
FUYUKIIII... OH, FUYUKIII...
THE NEW ISSUE OF YOUR OCCULT MAGAZINE IS HERE!

OH...
...REALLY ...?

C'MON... THERE'S A SPECIAL STORY ON "NEW CROP CIRCLES"!
UH... ...HUH...
"NEW DEVELOPMENT IN THE CAPTURE OF SKY FISH!" IT SAYS! AND...

UH... ...HUH...
!?
NO REACTION TO NEW OCCULT FINDINGS...? NO WAY!

WHAT... ISSSSSS... HAPPEN-INNNG?
KERORO KERO! ♪

DON'T COME IN WITHOUT KNOCKING !!!
ADESHIZUEEH?!!

URRR... OUCH...
HUH? IS MY ARM BENT THE WRONG WAY...?
ALL RIGHT, FUYUKI, WHAT'S THE MATTER?
SOMETHING WRONG?

WELL... THE OTHE DAY...
...I LOADED UP THE HOMEPAGE FOR THE CROP CIRCLE STUDY GROUP...
...THEN I RECEIVED AN EMAIL FROM AN ENGLISH COPYRIGHT ASSOCIATION!
"THE CROP CIRCLE IS THE COPYRIGHTED MATERIAL OF OUR ASSOCIATION," THEY SAID...

THEY MAKE THE CIRCLES, THEN SELL THEM TO THE JAPANESE MEDIA AND STUFF.
AFTER THAT...I JUST DON'T CARE ABOUT ANYTHING.
THE OCCULT IS JUST A BIG SCAM...

WHAT ARE YOU TALKING ABOUT? THE OCCULT CLEANS OUR HOUSE EVERY DAY!
Pain... slowly... spreading...
WHAT MORE COULD YOU ASK FOR?

WELL, THAT'S DIFFERENT. I'VE GOTTEN USED TO THE SERGEANT AND THOSE GUYS...

HUH...?

AND HE SAYS HE DOESN'T FEEL LIKE DOING ANYTHING!

OH, YOU MEAN FUYUKI?

SOUNDS LIKE A CASE OF MAY DISEASE.

MAY DISEASE?

RIGHT AROUND NOW, ALL THE NEW STUDENTS AND WORKERS HAVE SETTLED IN AND ARE TAKING A BREATHER...

...FREED FROM THEIR ENTRANCE EXAMS, OR THE BURDEN OF FINDING A JOB, PEOPLE EXPERIENCE A FEELING OF LET-DOWN...A LOSS OF PURPOSE.

THEY ALSO BECOME DISILLUSIONED... SEEING THE GAP BETWEEN REALITY AND WHAT THEY WERE HOPING FOR...

ALL THOSE THINGS COMBINED PUT PEOPLE IN A STATE OF MILD DEPRESSION.

MANGA CREATORS GET THAT WAY EVERY TIME THEY FINISH A BOOK.
IT SEEMS THAT INTROVERTED DREAMERS ARE ESPECIALLY PRONE TO IT.
ONLY BECAUSE THEY'RE UNHEALTHY TO BEGIN WITH.
I'LL NEVER UNDER-STAND IT!

DON
WORR
I'LL TAKE CARE OF IT. ♪
WINTER
FUYU-KIIII...
I'M COMING IN, OKAY? ♪
AW, WHAT'S WRONG? YOU SEEM DOWN.
WE'RE HAVING MOM'S SPECIAL DINNER TONIGHT!
UH...
...HUH...
HMM... THIS IS PRETTY SERIOUS.
IN THAT CASE...

HERE GOES!!!
WHUHHH?!
!?

Mmm... Mfff! Mgh....?!

MOM?! W-WHAT--?

HEL--

ALTHOUGH...

IT DOES SMELL NICE...AND IT'S KIND OF SOOTHING.

I DON'T KNOW WHY... BUT...

...IT MAKES ME FEEL... SAFE.

THAT'S MY KILLER LOCK, "LOVE'S SPECIAL HOLD." ♡

SEE? YOU'VE STILL GOT SOME SPIRIT LEFT IN YOU, FUYUKI!

GASP

URRR...

I'M GETTING JEALOUS.

ALL RIGHT, THEN! LET'S HAVE DINNER, OKAY?

KAY!!

WHAT AN AMAZING EFFECT!

MOM'S ILLER LOCK ALLY IS ILLER...

SORRY I MADE YOU WORRY.

GUESS I GOT TOO USED TO THINGS, AND FORGOT TO APPRECIATE WHAT WAS RIGHT IN FRONT OF ME.

WELL, YEAH. IF YOU CAN GET USED TO BEING WITH A BUNCH OF ALIENS...

...I GUESS I CAN SEE WHERE YOU'RE COMING FROM.
YOU HAD ALWAYS **DREAMED** OF MEETING ALIENS.
BUT IT TURNED OUT THOSE ALIENS WERE JUST GOOD-FOR-NOTHING, ORDINARY SLOBS...
I'D TAKE TO MY BED FROM DIS-APPOINT-MENT, TOO!
THAT'S QUITE ENOUGH, NATSUMI!
あはは
ははは
Ah ha ha ha ha ha!

"GOOD-FOR-NOTHING"? "ORDINARY"?!

YOU SHOULD TALK!!! TAKES ONE TO KNOW ONE!!!

HURK!

WHAT ARE YELLING ABOUT?! HAVE YOU LOST YOUR MIND?

GOOD-FOR-NOTHING... ORDI...GOOD-FOR-NOTHING AND ORDI... GOOD-FOR-NOTH...NOTH... NO...NO..

YOU HAVE NO IDEA WHAT I'M CAPABLE OF...I'LL SHOW YOU!!!

I WON'T FORGIVE. I CAN'T FORGIVE! STUPID, NO GOOD POKO-PENIANS!!

SER-GEANT?!

YOU INGRATE!! YOU FOOL!!!

DID I SAY SOMETHING BAD...?

DON'T WORRY ABOUT IT, FUYUKI!!!

BANG

CRASH

CLANG

OOF

BIFF

BAM

SER-GEANT?

KERORO PLATOON'S SECRET UNDERGROUND BASE

THIS IS... WOW!

May-zone 987230

COUTION

I'D BEEN **WONDERING** WHAT YOU WERE DOING THESE LAST FEW DAYS.
WHAT EXACTLY **IS IT**, KERORO?

THE KERORO OF DEATH!

死神化!

I GOT THIS IDEA WATCHING MASTER FUYUKI THE OTHER DAY.
I'M DEVELOPING AN ENERGY THAT WILL DEPRESS ALL POKO-PENIANS.
BY USING THIS, WE WILL LOWER THEIR TENSION-- AND WHEN IT REACHES BOTTOM, WE'LL HAVE COMPLETE CONTROL OVER THE PLANET!!

......
WHAT'S THE MATTER? HAVE A COMPLAINT, CORPORAL?

N-NO...IT'S JUST THAT THE OPERATION SEEMS SO CONCRETE... AND EFFECTIVE...
AND IT WASN'T SO BEFORE?!
WELL... NO...

THESE HINATAS... CALLING US "GOOD-FOR-NOTHING" AND "ORDINARY"!!
SOB
MY PRIDE WAS TORN INTO ITTY-BITTY PIECES THAT DAY!!
What a good-for-nothing guy! ♪
I even cried a little!

......
WHAT?! WHAT IS IT NOW?!

YOU HAVE... PRIDE ...?
OF COURSE I DO! WHAT?!
WELL... UH...

BY TH
WAY,
TAMAM
WHAT T
IS IT NO
MAY, SIR!
Gero Gerc
MAY...YES.
A GOOD NAM
A GOOD NAM
UNCLE...? ARE YOU FINALLY READY TO BE A TRUE VILLIAN?
KU, KU, KU, KU...

YES! I SHALL NAME IT "MAY-ZONE ENERGY"!
QUICKLY, EVERYONE! TO YOUR POSITIONS !!!
YESSIR!

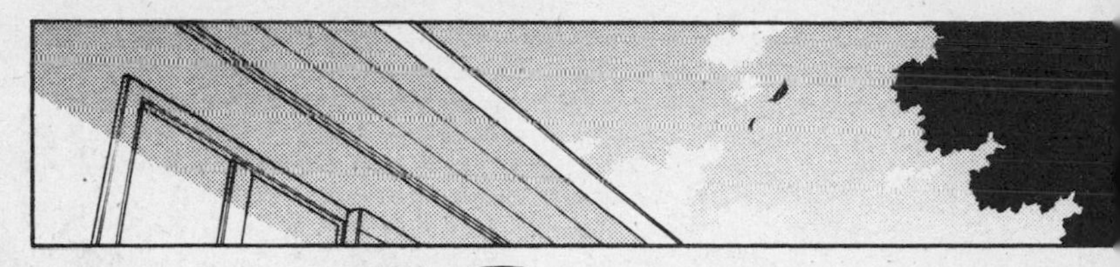

NATSU
WHERE
THE SE
GEANT
HOW SHOULD I KNOW?
In a blender, I hope.

I
HAVE
SEE
HIM IN
WHIL
SHUT UP AND GIVE ME A HAND!

SERGEANT...?
......

WOW!
AMAZINGLY EFFECTIVE!!

MAY-ZONE PRESSURIZED CONCENTRATION 73%...
ONLY THREE DAYS 'TIL CORE FORMATION! KU, KU, KU...

slump

TOO SLOW!! MAKE IT THREE HOURS!
KU, KU, KU. AYE, SIR...
HEY-- DON'T PUSH IT TOO HARD, KERORO!
I'LL SHOW THOSE POKO-PENIANS...
...WHAT KIND OF GOOD-FOR-NOTHING, ORDINARY ALIENS THEY'RE DEALING WITH!!
PSSS
CRACK

SEVERAL DAYS AFTER THE KERORO PLATOON...
...BEGAN TO DEVELOP THIS MYSTERIOUS ENERGY...

W-WHAT?! AN EARTH-QUAKE?!
DORORO ?!

ASSASSIN MILITARY TECHNIQUE: "I HAVE A HUNCH."
I FEEL SOME-THING'S HAPPENED TO THE CAPTAIN AND OTHERS!
WHAT?
WAIT--DORORO!!
FUYUKI?!
Emergency! Emergency!
Separation gate deployed. Entry is dangerous.
IT'S DANGEROUS FOR YOU TO GO ANY FURTHER.
FUYUKI, SIR...YOU OUGHT TO RETURN.
NO! I'M GOING, TOO!
!?

I HAVE TO APOLOGIZE TO THE SERGEANT...
THE SERGEANT IS NO LONGER AN OCCULT CURIOSITY... HE'S BECOME A REAL FRIEND! I WAS JUST...
?
TOUCHED
IN THAT CASE... I HAVE NO RIGHT TO STOP YOU.
HOWEVER-- YOU MUST PROTECT YOURSELF!!
OKAY. I WILL!
ARE YOU READY?!
Y-YES!!
レンタル*
HAAYA!

*rental

WE'RE GOING IN!!
SHING
WH-WHAT IS THIS?!
THERE'S BEEN AN ACCIDENT... THE AIR IS FILLED WITH AN UNKNOWN SUBSTANCE.
DORORO-- ARE YOU OKAY?!
SINCE I'M A SPECIAL ACTION SOLDIER, YOUR CONCERN IS NOT REQUIRED.
I CAN ADAPT TO ANY ENVIRONMENT.
But... what is this...?
MOA-CHAN?!

ARE YOU OKAY?! WHAT HAPPENED?!
...?
HUHHH?

UNCLE'S... MAY-ZONE...
......
......

Ohhh... who cares anyway...?
WHAAAAT?!

MOA-CHAN LOOKS... JUST LIKE...
...HOW I FELT A FEW DAYS AGO!!
Soooo tiiiired...
レンタル

HERE-- THE LAB'S OPERATION REPORT!

200x/5/xx
Began development of May-zone. Uncle's enthusiasm is so contagious... noisy, happy... how do you say... it's a picnic! ♪
With everyone's help, we will definitely succeed in creating this mysterious energy! Yeah!!
\(^o^)/ (Angol Moa)

MYSTERIOUS ENERGY? "MAY-ZONE?"
THAT MUST BE WHAT'S MAKING MOA-CHAN SO DEPRESSED!

SO... WHAT DID HAPPEN HERE?
LE 2
GIRORO-KUN?!

GIRORO-KUN!!
GIRORO-KUN! GET A HOLD OF YOURSELF.
I just don't care ...
...about anything... at all...

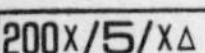
200X/5/XΔ

Keroro is making things happen for a change. I have no choice but to go along with it, even if the idea is a little ridiculous. And I might be imagining it...but I feel a little tired...

LEVEL.3

TA-MAMA?!!

huff huff

Someone... please... turn the page for me...

200X/5/XO

Phaaaah... So sleepy... So tired... So much hassle... Could someone put a piece of candy in my mouth?

2003/5/△△
Ku
SER-GEANT!! SER-GEANT--?!
Check OK!
Check OK!
Check OK!
THEY ALL LOOK AS THOUGH THEIR SOULS HAVE GONE FROM THEIR BODIES...
THAT MUST BE THE EFFECT OF MAY-ZONE!!
IF THIS WERE TO LEAK INTO EARTH'S ATMO-SPHERE...
...THE RESULTS WOULD BE CATA-STROPHIC!!
MUMMY... WHY IS EVERYONE ON THIS PLANET LOOKING DOWN?
BECAUSE EVERYONE HERE IS DEPRESSED.
.......!!!
WE MUST PUT A STOP TO THIS...
...NO MATTER WHAT!!!
MAY-ZONE

Emergency!
Emergency!
Control device did not foresee current scenario. Emergency shutdown imminent.
mergency!
......
W-WHAT IS THIS?!
ASSAS-SIN MAGIC!
PPRAISAL VISION!!!

MAY-ZONE GENERATING CORE. CODE NAME: "SATSUKI MAY." PHYSICAL MANIFESTATION OF THE SUPER-PRESSURIZED MAY-ZONE.
THROUGH ABSORPTION OF SYNTHETIC PERSONALITY TRAITS FROM THE MANAGING OS AND ACCUMULATION OF SOLID MATERIAL FROM PERIPHERY DEVICES, AN INDEPENDENT LIFE FORM WAS FORMED.
I AM MAY-ZONE... ALL WILL FALL BEFORE ME.
EARTH WILL BECOME A PARADISE... WITH NO ENERGY FOR CONFLICT.
Emergency!
Activate control device manually.
!!
DORORO! THE CONTROL DEVICE!
UNDERSTOOD!
THERE IT IS!!
WHAT?!
IT'S ALREADY WORKING ON A GLOBAL SCALE??!

K-KERORO-KUN?!
Let it go, man...
Let's get wasted...
!?
SERGEANT!!
S-START THE DEVICE WITHOUT ME!
O-OKAY!!
I MUST SAVE THE SERGEANT...
...AND THE EARTH...
I WILL NOT...
...LET YOU INTERFERE...
MASTER FUYUKI!!!

NOW YO
TOO, AR
MAY-ZON
CAPTIVE
YOU CANN
MOVE A
LONGER

NO...

WELL,
NO
MATTER...

EVEN IF I DIE...
THERE WILL
BE OTHERS...

Control
device
activated.

WE-WE
ARE
SAVED!

BUT...
HOW?

MASTER
FUYUKI!!
HEH
HEH
HEH...

I SEE!
SINCE YOU HAD ALREADY HAD MAY DISEASE, MASTER FUYUKI...
...YOU CLEARLY DEVELOPED AN IMMUNITY TO IT!
You think so?
Ah ha ha ha...
I'M SORRY, SER-GEANT...
NO--SO AM I. I TOOK THINGS TOO SERIOUSLY AND CAUSED A BIG NUISANCE...
HUH? SHE SAID SORRY?

WELL, I WAS THE ONE WHO SAID THOSE UNKIND THINGS...
...SO THIS TIME, NO PUNISHMENT! YOU CAN SKIP ALL YOUR CHORES FOR ONE WHOLE WEEK, IF YOU WISH!
TAKE IT EASY FOR ONCE!
YAHOO! YES! YES!!
A VACA-TION!!

AND SO KERORO PLATOON RECEIVED A SPECIAL HOLIDAY... IN STARK CONTRAST FROM ALL THE HARSH WORK THEY HAD PREVIOUSLY ENDURED...
....
huff huff
...AND WENT RIGHT BACK TO SUFFERING FROM MAY DISEASE!
TO BE CONTINUED

STU-PID-FROOGGGG!
CLEAN THE YARD, OKAY?!
Gero?! BUT I'M IN THE MIDDLE OF MASKING THE CURVED AREA!
QUIET, FREE-LOADER!
GAH! MASTER NATSUMI! SUCH A WENCH!
EVERY OTHER WORD SHE UTTERS IS "FREE-LOADER."
I'll help, too!
Myeh mveh myeh. "You're from Planet Free-load"!
LOOK-- LOOK, UNCLE!
THERE'S SOMETHING STRANGE OVER THERE-- LIKE, THE WONDERS OF NATURE?
HUH... THAT...?
ENCOUNTER LXI SWALLOW THIS! AN ANNUAL INVASION

ENCOUNTER LXI SWALLOW THIS! AN ANNUAL INVASION

Gero...? IT APPEARS TO BE A PILE OF DIRT.
CLEARLY THE WORK OF SOME NEIGH-BORHOOD BRATS!
GREAT, GREAT. MORE WORK FOR ME ...
Sigh...
I JUST CAN'T UNDER-STAND WHAT GOES ON IN THE MIND OF A BRAT LIKE THAT!
※ IMPRESSIVE? OR NOT?
KIEEEEH! ULTIMATE GUTTERING BROOM ATTACK!!!
THAT OLD ATTACK? IT JUST LOOKS LIKE THERE ARE MANY BROOMS.
STOP IT, SERGEANT!!
!?
AAAAH!! OUCH! OUCH! OUCH!
Master Fukkie?
HOW IS IT THAT MY OWN TRICK IS ATTACKING ME...?

THIS IS A SWALLOW'S NEST.
SWAL-LOW?
IT'S A BIRD THAT TRAVELS TO JAPAN EVERY YEAR AT ABOUT THIS TIME TO HAVE CHICKS.
SWALLOWS ARE HARD-WORKING AND CUTE. THEY'RE VERY POPULAR!

SO DON'T BOTHER IT, OKAY?
A-OKAY!

HARD-WORKING? POPULAR? ANNOYING, THAT'S WHAT IT IS!
IN A WAY, IT'S ALSO A FREE-LOADER... AND A WICKED ONE AT THAT!

I OBJECT, MASTER FUYUKI!!!
!
HARDWORKING, CUTE, POPULAR, AND A FREELOADER...
こたえて
IF I MAY SAY SO, IT'S EXACTLY THE SAME AS ME!!
SO WHY IS IT TREATED SO DIFFERENTLY FROM ME?! WHY IS THAT?!

IT'S NOT FAIR! IT'S NOT FAIR!
WELL...I'M NOT QUITE SURE HOW TO ANSWER THAT...
CLACK
Wahh! Wahh!

I NEED TO KNOW!!

OH, FUYUKI--YOU'RE HOME.
HEHGUBEH!
BONK
MASTER NATSUMI. I'M STUCK. I'M STUCK!
GOWAAH... CRUSH... CRUSHED ...!
LOOK, NATSUMI!
WOW--HOW CUTE! A SWALLOW'S NEST! ♪
THE SWALLOWS HAVE COME AGAIN THIS YEAR, FLYING THROUGH SKIES FAR AND HIGH...
THROUGH RAIN, THROUGH WIND, THROUGH STORM AND SEA...
HMM... I MUST BE A POET!
YOU.
DON'T EVEN THINK ABOUT TOUCHING THIS NEST!!
Gero... Gero...?

DON'T YOU THINK THERE SHOULD BE LIMITS TO SUCH UNREASONABLE BEHAVIOR?!!
EVERYONE, NOW!

......
I CAN TELL YOU THAT.
GO ON. GO ON.

I SEE NO DIFFERENCE BETWEEN ME AND THIS SO-CALLED SWALLOW!
I DEMAND A REASONABLE EXPLANATION. GAH-- I SWEAR!!

IT COMES DOWN TO THE FACT THAT THE SWALLOW HAS CHARM ...
Yes, yes?

...AND YOU DON'T.
THAT'S ALL.

I'M LOSING IT!! I TELL YOU, I HAVE LOST IT!!
THERE'S NO TELLING WHAT I MIGHT DO NOW!!!

YES... I WILL ELIMINATE THESE UNWANTED VISITORS.
THE KEY WILL BE TO MAKE SURE IT LOOKS LIKE AN ACCIDENT...
ACTING AS IF HE'S LOST IT, THE SERGEANT IS ACTUALLY CALCULATING HIS NEXT MOVE!
うっしっし
HEY, WAIT.
WHAT ARE YOU DOING WITH THAT BALL?

WHAT? THIS?
WELL, IT'S LIKE THIS! THIS BALL... WHICH SOME BRATS KICKED IN OVER THE FENCE... UNFORTUNATELY HIT THE NEST... AND...!
Yee Hee Hee! Yee Hee Hee!
GRAB
?

YOU MUST REALLY LIKE SOCCER TO PLAY AT THIS TIME OF DAY.
SO. THIS LITTLE LADY WILL SHOW YOU HOW TO PLAY REAL GOOD. ♡

KICK
KICK

THE NEXT DAY...

chirp chirp chirp

I FEEL DIFFERENTLY ABOUT SOCCER NOW...
...BUT IT DID MAKE ME DO SOME SERIOUS SOUL-SEARCHING.

chirp chirp chirp

MORE COMMUNICATION! SAY IT OUT LOUD!!
Let's go!
POKOPENIANS AND SWALLOWS, LET'S ALL UNDERSTAND EACH OTHER!!
To Spaceship Earth-- Bridge Number Three!
SEEMS HE WAS HIT IN THE RIGHT PLACE!

BOING

GOOD MORNING, MASTER NATSUMI!!
OH--MORNING! DID YOU HAVE TIME LAST NIGHT TO THINK ABOUT WHAT YOU DID?
OH, YES!! SO HARD THAT MY HEAD ALMOST CRACKED OPEN!!
IN THAT CASE, YOU'RE EXCUSED. ♪
......?
WHAAAAAATTT?!!
?
MASTER NATSUMI!! W-WHAT IS THAT ON YOUR HEAD?
HUH? NOTHING ...
Yawwwn...
GOOD MORNING, NATSUMI, SERGEANT...
GOOD MORNING, FUYU--
WHAT THE--?!!
?

WHAT'S WRONG? WHY THE FUNNY FACE?
AH HA HA. HE ALWAYS LOOKS LIKE THAT!
M...
MAYBE IT'S IN STYLE?
RUSTLE
IT'S THAT TIME OF THE YEAR...WHEN THE EARLY SUMMER BREEZE FEELS COMFORTABLE ON ONE'S SKIN...
FINE WEATHER TODAY. NOTHING UNUSUAL FROM THE EAST, WEST, NORTH OR SOU--
TMP

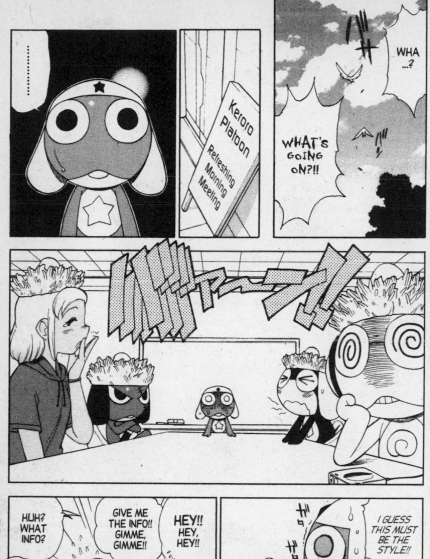

WHA ...?
WHAT's GOING ON?!!
Keroro Platoon
Refreshing Morning Meeting
....

I GUESS THIS MUST BE THE STYLE!!
I'VE FALLEN BEHIND IN THE TRENDS!!
HEY!! HEY, HEY!!
GIVE ME THE INFO!! GIMME, GIMME!!
HUH? WHAT INFO?
WHERE ALL DID YOU GET THESE?!
PLEASE-- DON'T LEAVE ME OUT!!
(DESPERATE!)

OH, DORORO-- YOU HAVEN'T GOT ONE YET? BOTH OF US... SO BEHIND THE TIMES...
KERORO-KUN!!
What are you talking about?
SOMETHING VERY SERIOUS IS HAPPENING IN THE HINATA HOUSEHOLD!!
HUH?
THAT POPULAR, HUH...
WHAT ARE YOU SAYING, KERORO-KUN?
I'M DETECTING ANTI-BARRIER WAVES FROM IT!!
WHAT ?!

COULD IT BE...AN INVADING ENEMY?!
WE HAVE BEEN... COLONIZED ?!
SQUAK
SCREE
SKRAWK
squak
skree
peep

CRACK
CRACK
SCREECH
HUH?!!
chirp
chirp
!?
MEOWWW!
WHOAAA... WH-WHAT IS IT?!
cheep
peep
cheep

I'M SORRY. FOR A LITTLE WHILE, WE LIVED ON YOU.
BUT NOW, THANKS TO YOU, MY CHILDREN HAVE BEEN BORN SAFE AND SOUND.

WE SWALLOW-NIANS TRAVEL THROUGH-OUT THE UNIVERSE LIKE THIS.
WE MUST LEAVE FOR THE NEXT PLANET RIGHT AWAY.

CHILDREN, LET US THANK THIS PLANET--AND THE PEOPLE WHO CALL IT HOME.

THANK YOU!

THANKS!

THANK YOU!

THANK YOU!

THANK YOU!

ARIGATO!

THANKS A LOT!

HMM...

SO THAT WAS ALL...?

FOR A WHILE THERE, WE OURSELVES...
...WERE COMPLETELY, THOROUGHLY INVADED!

HEY! MY BODY FEELS INCREDIBLY LIGHT AND AGILE NOW!
ME, TOO! MY MIND IS AS CLEAR AS A BELL!
I FEEL FANTASTIC!!! ♪
THAT WAS A MODEL INVASION.
THE SWALLOWNIANS' PARASITISM IS SAID TO HAVE THE SIDE EFFECT OF LEAVING ITS HOSTS IN TIP-TOP CONDITION!

HEY, YOU!
COME BACK AGAIN WHEN YOUR KIDS ARE BIGGER!
AND NEXT TIME--PLEASE LIVE ON ME, TOO!!

BZZZ BZZZ
LOOK, LOOK--ISN'T THIS THE HIPPEST?!
IT'S THE NEXT TRENDY THING!
DORORO'S APPRAISAL VISION: "DEADLY BEE"--INVADING PARASITIC ALIEN. BARB AT THE END OF ITS BELLY CAN KILL AN AFRICAN ELEPHANT WITH A SINGLE STING.
TO BE CONTINUED

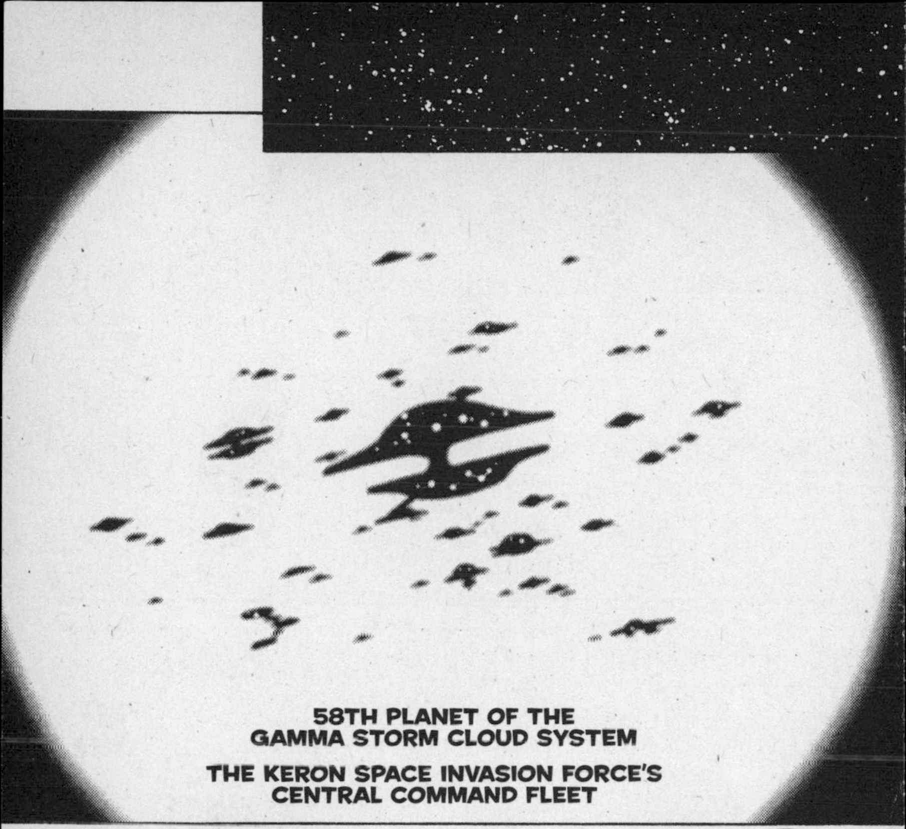

58TH PLANET OF THE GAMMA STORM CLOUD SYSTEM

THE KERON SPACE INVASION FORCE'S CENTRAL COMMAND FLEET

CONFIRM RETURN AND COLLECTION OF "TYPE K-66 NO. 315" AND "K-66X5-2301V3" PLATOON.
COMMENCE MEMORY ERASURE AND PSYCHIATRIC CLEANSING.

ENCOUNTER 54.5
THE WORLD'S SMALLEST INVASION: THE LOST EPISODE

PSYCHIATRIC LOAD VALUE IS REGISTERING AT OVER 100 TIMES THAT OF AN ORDINARY KERONIAN.
EVEN THAT IS ONLY HALF THE AVERAGE VALUE OF A POKO-PENIAN...
ウォン
フォン

I GUESS THAT EXPLAINS WHY POKOPEN...
フォン…
ウォン
...REMAINS NEUTRAL GROUND...

WE HAVE ALREADY ALERTED THE PLATOON MEMBERS ABOUT THE POSSIBILITY OF CANCEL-ING THIS OPERATION.
IT CAN'T BE HELPED...

OH-- MASTER FUYUKI!!
I GOT A NEW COSMIC INSECT. WOULD YOU LIKE TO SEE IT?
HYAAAA-- MASTER NATSUMI?!
I DIDN'T MEAN TO-- PLEASE-- FORGIVE ME--!!

OH... HUH...?
MASTER NATSUMI?
MASTER FUYUKI?

FU... YU...

KEROOOOOO!!!!

BLUB

BLIBBLE? BUBBUB... HUBUB BUBB... (OH MY, GIRORO!)

BUBB BUBBLE RUBADUB DUB? (WHAT KIND OF ACCIDENT DID YOU CAUSE TODAY?)

WAKE UP, IDIOT! WE'RE ESCAPING RIGHT AWAY!!

I'VE SECURED A SPACE-SHIP--HURRY!
THANKS, GARURU!
Garu, Garu... YOU'RE PRETTY DESPARATE, GIRORO.
DID YOU FIND SOME-THING ON POKOPEN... OR SOME-ONE?
SH-SHUT UP!!

KU, KU, KU... HERE THEY COME...

THIS WAY!!

I'VE RE-WRITTEN ALL OF THEIR MEMORIES ...

KU!

EXCELLENT JOB, KULULU!!

WE SHALL RETURN TO THE FRONT-LINE!!

OPERATION: POKOPEN INVASION IS STILL IN PROGRESS!!!

in a stupor...

?

FULL SPEED AHEAD !!!

DESTINATION: POKOPEN !!!!

CAPTURE OF ALTERED MEMORIES SUCCESSFUL.

Only Sergeant Major Kululu would be capable of such a thing...

WHAT NOW, COLONEL?

THEY SAY THEY'LL DO IT THEMSELVES.

AND I SEE NO REASON TO STOP THEM.

TO BE CONTINUED

JAPAN STAFF

CREATOR
MINE YOSHIZAKI

BACKGROUNDS
OYSTER

FINISH
GOMOKU AKATSUKI
ROBIN TOKYO
TONMI NARIHARA

CONTINUED IN VOLUME 8

THE GIRL FROM NONTORUMA*

* A play on the word "Nonmruto," which in *Ultraman* was used to mean the indigenous people of Earth.

WHAT'S WRONG, NATSUMI?

SLUG!! SLUG! SLUG!

I HATE THEM! I HATE THEM! GROSS! GROSS! GROSS! GROSS!

THEY'RE SLIMY, THEY'RE SLIPPERY AND THEY'RE SQUISHY!

JUST LOOKING AT THEM MAKES MY WHOLE BODY WEAK!

AND I TOUCHED ONE!

OHHH! GROSS, GROSS, GROSS!!! I TOUCHED ONE!

HERE, FUYUKI-- YOU TAKE CARE OF THIS!!

PLANT ONE EVERY TWO INCHES, OKAY?

Slug-A-Way

TOKYOPOP PRESS

LOS ANGELES • TOKYO • LONDON • HAMBURG

Gero Gero Gero!
ALLOW ME TO INTRODUCE MY "ANTI-NATSUMI BIOLOGICAL WEAPON"...
...A GENETICALLY ENGINEERED SUPER-SLUG FROM THE TWIN LANDS OF "WET" AND "SLIMY"...
I GIVE YOU... WET-TRAMAN!!
THIS EARLY MODEL, KNOWN FOR THE SUNKEN AREA AROUND ITS MOUTH, WAS LATER CALLED "A-TYPE."
SL--
SLUG?!

NEXT IN VOLUME 8 OF

SGT FROG
KERORO GUNSOU

IN STORES THE MONTH OF MAY!

N-NO...
MY WHOLE BODY...IS... WILTING...

SLUG FEST!

A Slimy Stymie

The Sergeant's biggest menace has been Natsumi, Earth's first line of defense. But Sgt. Keroro has finally discovered her one weakness: soggy, sticky slugs. The Sergeant develops his ultimate weapon against Natsumi--***Wet-traman***, a mucous monster with 1,000 times the power of a garden-variety slug!! And the anthropomorphic antics are only just beginning. Keroro is off to the zoo to recruit reinforcements for his platoon, and he takes Kururu's latest animal-altering invention with him!

SOKORA REFUGEES
The savior of a world without hope faces her greatest challenge: Cleavage!

STOP!

This is the back of the book.
You wouldn't want to spoil a great ending!

This book is printed "manga-style," in the authentic Japanese right-to-left format. Since none of the artwork has been flipped or altered, readers get to experience the story just as the creator intended. You've been asking for it, so TOKYOPOP® delivered: authentic, hot-off-the-press, and far more fun!

DIRECTIONS

If this is your first time reading manga-style, here's a quick guide to help you understand how it works.

It's easy... just start in the top right panel and follow the numbers. Have fun, and look for more 100% authentic manga from TOKYOPOP®!